Studies on the Chinese Market Economy Series

Reforming China's State-Owned Enterprises

Chief Editors:
Gao Shangquan *and* Chi Fulin

FOREIGN LANGUAGES PRESS   BEIJING

First Edition 1997

The project is aided by
(Hainan) China Foundation for Reform and Development Research.

ISBN 7-119-00300-3

© Foreign Languages Press, Beijing, China, 1997

Published by Foreign Languages Press
24 Baiwanzhuang Road, Beijing 100037, China

Distributed by China International Book Trading Corporation

35 Chegongzhuang Xilu, Beijing 100044, China
P.O. Box 399, Beijing, China

Printed in the People's Republic of China

Editor's Note

Reform of state-owned enterprises has always been an important element of China's overall economic reform. At present, reform of the state-owned enterprise system is a major and crucial aspect of China's shift from a planned economy to a market economy, and accordingly has commanded widespread attention. Since its founding, the China (Hainan) Institute for Reform and Development has taken reform of state-owned enterprises as a major issue for study and has developed many new ideas and perspectives, resulting in rapid progress. On this foundation, in October 1994 the China (Hainan) Institute for Reform and Development, along with the China Economic System Reform Association, the United Nations Development Planning Office and the German Technology Cooperation Company, jointly sponsored the "International Forum on China's Reform of State-Owned Enterprises." The forum lasted three days and was attended by the leaders of government departments, scientific and academic experts, leaders of provincial and municipal committees for restructuring the economic systems, managers from large and medium-sized enterprises and economists from Taiwan. Also attending were officials from the United Nations, the International Monetary Fund, and economists from France, Holland, Hungary, the United States, Australia, Chile, the Republic of Korea, and Vietnam. Reform of state-owned enterprises was the focus of the discussions which were both extensive and thorough, resulting in many observations and constructive criticism. In April 1995, the China (Hainan) Institute for Reform and Development and the United Nations Development Planning Office convened the "International Forum on Reform of State-Owned Enterprises and Comparative Management in the Asia-Pacific Region," which was attended by over 40 experts and officials from China and abroad. Again, many important views and opinions were exchanged. This book was compiled on the basis of research done by the China (Hainan) Institute for Reform and Development, and according to discussions and lectures at the two forums as well as additional reference sources. We would like to express our sincere thanks to all those, from both China and abroad, whose views are represented on these pages.

This book does not supply a single answer or final conclusion to the important questions facing China's state-owned enterprises, but it does aim to provide readers with the ideas, perspectives, and views of domestic and international scholars in the hope that readers may glean the essentials and thereby gain some insight into the situation.

This book was edited by Gao Shangquan and Chi Fulin and was written by Sun Xiuping. Workers in the research, information, and other departments of the China (Hainan) Institute for Reform and Development made great contributions to this book, and to all of them we express our respect and thanks.

Errors or inconsistencies may appear in this book and we welcome corrections from our readers.

Editors

Contents

Chapter I
Reform of State-Owned Enterprises: The Crux of China's Economic Structural Reform   1
   I. State-Owned Enterprises: The Current Situation and Outlook   1
   II. Problems of Innovation Within the Chinese Enterprise System   8

Chapter II
Basic Thoughts on the Transformation Period for State-owned Enterprises   18
   I. Enlivening the State-Owned Economy as a Whole   18
   II. Creating a Modern Enterprise System—the Basic Task for Transforming the Economic System   21
   III. Measures to Deepen the Reform of State-Owned Enterprises   37

Chapter III
Reform of the Property Rights System: A Breakthrough in the Reform of State-Owned Enterprises   46
   I. Making Clear Property Relations for the Transition to a Modern Enterprise System   46
   II. What Are the Independent Property Rights of the Enterprise's Legal Person?   59
   III. The Issue of the Central and Local Publicly Owned Assets   66
   IV. Establishing the Property Rights of the Labor Force Under the Socialist Market Economy   72
   V. Property Rights Market: Advancing the Circulation and Reorganization of Property Rights   80

Chapter IV
The Transformation of State-Owned Enterprises Under a Corporate System — 85
  I. Reform of State-Owned Enterprises of Various Types and a Model for Corporate System Transformation — 85
  II. The Chinese Style of the Western Modern Corporate System — 105
  III. Readjustment of the Enterprises Structure and Organization of Corporate Groups — 113
  IV. Standard Operation of State-Owned Stocks and Standardization of the Corporate System — 137

Chapter V
Reorganization of State-Owned Enterprises and Their Liabilities — 151
  I. Significance and Methods of Reorganizing State-Owned Enterprises — 151
  II. The Necessity of Reorganizing the Liabilities of State-Owned Enterprises — 160
  III. Methods and Measures for Reorganizing the Liabilities of State-Owned Enterprises — 166

Chapter VI
Reconfiguration of State-Owned Assets Management — 182
  I. The Present Situation and Problems of State-Owned Assets Management in China — 182
  II. The Reconstruction of the State-Owned Assets Management System — 185
  III. Constructing the Operating System for State-Owned Assets with the Establishment of State-Owned Holding Companies as the Key — 193
  IV. Optimum Results for State-Owned Assets: Reallocation of State-Owned Assets — 203

Chapter VII
Separation of Government Administration from Management: The Key to Changing the State-Owned Enterprise System — 207
  I. The Roots of the Deep Contradictions in the Reform of the

    China's Economic System   207
  II. The Government Functions and Responsibilities under the Market Economy   212
  III. A Design for the Separation of Government Administration from Enterprise Management and the Reform of Organizations   215

Chapter VIII
Eetablishing a Mechanism for the Scientific Management of State-Owned Enterprises   218

  I. The Basic Idea for Reform of the Internal Management of State-Owned Enterprises   218

  II. The Key to Scientific Management: Perfecting the Company's Corporate Administrative Structure   222

  III. The Modern Enterprise System Calls for Modern Entrepreneurs   223

Chapter I
Reform of State-Owned Enterprises: The Crux of China's Economic Structural Reform

I. State-Owned Enterprises: The Current Situation and Outlook

At present, state-owned enterprises still play an important role in the Chinese national economy. This role can be seen mainly in four aspects. First, state-owned enterprises still make up a considerable part of the economy; as a proportion of the gross national product (GNP) they represent 35-40 percent. Second, a large proportion of industry consists of state-owned enterprises. Excluding enterprises below the township level, the number of state-owned enterprises comes close to 50 percent of all enterprises. They still comprise about 40 percent of the total enterprises including those below the township level, while township enterprises take up 50 percent, and foreign-invested enterprises (Chinese-foreign joint ventures, Chinese-foreign cooperative enterprises and wholly owned foreign enterprises), individual enterprises and privately operated enterprises, about 10 percent each. Third, the heart of the national economy, such as infrastructure, energy, transportation, public utilities, and other backbone industries are all state-owned. As non-state-owned enterprises in these areas are small in number, the development of township enterprises, industry and the entire economy would be impossible without the dominant role of state-owned enterprises. Fourth, state-owned enterprises provide more than 60 percent of all state revenue, making them the state's preeminent source of income.

On the other hand, many outstanding problems exist in state-owned enterprises today, some of which have become a major encumbrance to Chinese society. This is primarily apparent in the fact that many state-owned enterprises show poor financial returns and have incurred large debts. According to 1994 statistics, nearly 40 percent of all state-owned enterprises were operating in the red. Moreover, these figures were generated before the new accounting system was fully in place and do not reflect the whole picture. Also, the input-output ratio of state-owned enterprises is very low. Over 70 percent of 1993's fixed assets and capital loans went to state-owned enterprises, but the proportion held by state-owned enterprises in the growth sector of the national economy was only 20 percent and estimates for 1994 are that they won't even reach that high. This is all to say that the main force of economic growth is generated by non-state-owned enterprises. In 1994 the economy grew at a rate of 11.8 percent, but the growth of state-owned enterprises was only 2 to 3 percent at most. In the 15 years since the initiation of reform and opening to the outside world, only 12.2 percent of the net output value of state-owned enterprises was a result of increased financial returns while 87.8 percent was due to increased investment. In other words, state-owned enterprises basically rely on increasing investment. Development in the United States was equivalent to that of China in the past 40 years: The proportion of growth due to increased investment amounted to slightly over 40 percent, whereas growth from increased returns reached 54 percent. This calculation is determined from overall growth figures. If calculated only on the basis of profits, the results are much the same. The proportion of increased profits of China's state-owned enterprises stemming from increased financial returns is less than 20 percent; from increased investment, more than 80 percent. American increases resulting from greater investment amounted to less than 35 percent, whereas that from increased returns was more than 65 percent. This illustrates that operation in state-owned enterprises is far from ideal, and that in fact this has already become a problem that must be solved in the implementation of a healthy economic cycle.

CHAPTER I CRUX OF CHINA'S ECONOMIC STRUCTURAL REFORM

Currently, the Chinese economy is indeed in good shape, but several prominent problems do exist. Moreover, they exist at a quite fundamental level in five areas:

The first problem is inflation which remains high to the present day. The 1994 annual plan and the resolution passed by the National People's Congress aimed at bringing inflation down below the double-digit mark (or below 10 percent), but inflation that year was 21.7 percent. Estimates for 1995 also say it is improbable that inflation will fall below 10 percent, with the lowest figure projected at 13 percent, and some predicting as high as 15 percent. This is higher than in the majority of countries throughout the world.

The second problem is employment. According to statistics urban unemployment was 2.3 percent in 1993 and 2.9 percent in 1994, and estimates for 1995 do not exceed 4 percent. These are very low figures, basically full employment. However, these statistics are incomplete and are missing two important elements. First, urban state-owned enterprises currently have some 20 to 30 million latently unemployed workers. Second, in the countryside a surplus labor force of some 100 million are in need of employment. The surge of peasants coming into the cities each year after the Spring Festival is a case in point. Because the economic situation is now quite good, employment opportunities in the cities are plentiful and most people who have already arrived from the countryside are able to settle down, or at least make ends meet. As for the other 100 million, if only half of them or less, say 30 to 50 million came to the cities, the cities would be overwhelmed, making it extremely difficult to maintain social order.

The third problem is the relationship between urban and rural areas. Since the start of reform both the countryside and cities have been developing, and the standard of living in both has been on the rise. But the cities have developed a bit quicker than the countryside. As a result, the disparity between urban and rural areas and between workers and peasants has shown signs of broadening in recent years.

The fourth problem lies in the economic structure. In general, in China's current economic structure the processing industry is developing too quickly while energy resources, transportation, and the infrastructure and relatively backward. These factors place major restraints on rapid development of the national economy.

Fifth is the problem of state-owned enterprises. State-owned enterprises are inefficient and are burdened with large debt and a shortage of capital. Quite a number of them have difficulty in maintaining normal operations. According to a survey done in August, 1994, out of 1,320 state-owned large and medium-sized state-owned enterprises in Liaoning Province, only 10.4 percent could truly be said to be in good shape, and even these were not without problems. Unless rectified in time, these enterprises are always in danger of decline. Relatively successful enterprises accounted for 22.1 percent; enterprises with major difficulties and large gaps between assets and liabilities, yet which can still be saved, amounted to 49.7 percent. Those unable to be saved accounted for close to 18 percent, and the number nearing bankruptcy was estimated at over 10 percent (some say around 15 percent). A good portion of these enterprises are getting worse and won't be able to solve their problems. For instance, of the third category (49.7 percent) it is certain that a large proportion will slowly move toward bankruptcy. Therefore, although state-owned enterprises serve an important function, they have become our "heart disease." On the one hand state-owned enterprises are of major importance; on the other hand, they are a national burden. In addition, these two facets are continually evolving: the pillar-like function may possibly decrease while the burdens progressively increase.

If the aforementioned five problems are not resolved it will be impossible for China's economy to move toward prosperity and stability. But many problems remain to be solved before these difficulties can be overcome. Moreover, the measures adopted frequently clash with one another. For example, in order to control inflation, China must control demand and currency, and compress the scale and speed of capital construction. Also, employment problems must be faced with specific goals and time-

CHAPTER I CRUX OF CHINA'S ECONOMIC STRUCTURAL REFORM

tables. Problems in the countryside require increased state financing or it will be impossible to resolve them. Energy, transportation, and infrastructure problems too need definite sizing and income for resolution. All these requirements hold even more true for state-owned enterprises.

The key to economic reform lies in reform of these state-owned enterprises. It means that if reform of state-owned enterprises can be firmly grasped, their economic benefits and wealth will increase. Even if investment remains at the present level, social wealth will increase greatly. Because the latent potential of state-owned enterprises is great, and other problems can then be readily solved.

As for inflation, if the economic benefits of state-owned enterprises grow, inflation—particularly the inflation resulted from an increase in production cost—can be absorbed, preventing rises in production costs being passed on to the price of the finished product. This is a very workable theory: Both post-World War II Germany and Japan since the 1970s had success by following this model.

By raising the economic benefits of state-owned enterprises, not only will inflation be controlled, but workers' incomes will rise as well, improving their ability to withstand inflation. Moreover, the state's financial revenue will increase, the scale of construction will expand, growth will quicken, and unemployment will be relieved.

This also applies to the countryside: Once state-owned enterprises are rectified and state financial revenues rise, the state can then assist or even subsidize agriculture. In developed countries the urban-rural gap has been overcome not only by increasing agricultural production, but also by state subsidies to agriculture as is the case when the state purchases agricultural products at high prices and then exports them at low prices. How large should these types of subsidies be? Japan, the United States and the Europe Economic Community (EEC) provide three examples. The proportion of farmers' net agricultural income coming from all subsidies amounts to 30 percent in the United States, 50 percent in the EEC, and 70 percent in Japan. That is to say that, for every dollar that a Japanese farmer takes in, 70 cents come from the government. And where does the government get this money? Because of the high economic returns from urban enterprises and industry, these revenues can be transferred from secondary and tertiary industries. China's greatest difficulty lies in just this area: Not only is the farming sector huge, making it impossible for the state to subsidize it, but industries aren't very profitable, leaving the state no financial leeway. Thus, it is extremely difficult for the state to increase agricultural subsidies at all. This means that if profitability of state-owned enterprises is not turned around, the urban-rural gap will be very difficult to narrow.

These conditions apply as well to the infrastructure. Currently, investment in state-owned enterprises makes up a large percentage of total investment, and the proportion of the state's financial revenue derived from state-owned enterprises is also quite large. If revenues from state-owned enterprises rise, the state's revenues will increase as well and infrastructure construction will be correspondingly strengthened. In addition, if the economic benefits of state-owned enterprises increase, their own problems will be solved as well. Therefore, deepening reform of state-owned enterprises is a task of the utmost urgency.

China wishes to establish a complete socialist market economic system, so reform can be seen at three levels: Enterprises, the market, and the macroeconomy. These three levels interact with and restrain each other, and all are necessary. Since the initiation of reform and opening to the outside world, the growth and development of the market has been relatively speedy and successful because of China's persistence in turning to the market. However, development among these three levels has been uneven. Before 1994, the development of state enterprises and the macroeconomy was rather stagnant. Since 1994, owing to major macroeconomic reforms in state financial administration, taxation, finance, investment, and the merger of the two foreign exchange rates, the sluggish condition at the macroeconomic level has been transformed. A year after implementation, rectification of financial administration, taxation, and the merger of the exchange

CHAPTER I CRUX OF CHINA'S ECONOMIC STRUCTURAL REFORM

rates have been essentially completed. But progress in the reform of finance and investment has been comparatively slow, especially in relation to several major financial reform goals. The operation of specialized banks as enterprises and the marketization of loan interest rates, for example, have not really been started yet. It is mainly because the seriously stagnant reform of state-owned enterprises cannot meet the demands of the above financial reforms. If this situation persists, there may be continued restraint and non-completion of financial reforms, or macroeconomic reform may be forced to make all kinds of allowances and accommodations. This not only may wreck what advances have been made, but may seriously delay progress in the construction of the new economic system, and thereby affect and restrict further economic development. Therefore, reform of state-owned enterprises must be undertaken as a matter of utmost importance and a pressing requirement for the nation.

Once again, state-owned enterprises are now facing contradictions at the deepest levels—the conflicts between the introduction of market mechanisms and the serious restrictions of the traditional system. More than a decade of market-oriented reform has established market mechanisms while phasing out a large portion of mandatory planning and essentially freeing the price structure. This has caused enterprises—state-owned and otherwise—to turn toward the market and compete equally with one another. The traditional administrative management system has not yet been reformed or abandoned; enterprises are still, to a large degree, subordinate to the government; the relations of property rights have not been straightened out; and the status of enterprises as legal entities has not been clearly defined. Add to this the incompleteness of the market setup and market mechanisms. The result is that state-owned enterprises face major restrictions when competing in the market. At the same time, state-owned enterprises are in an unequal competitive position with non-state-owned enterprises. Deep contradictions within the system are at the root of their problems.

Along with the acceleration of marketization and internationalization of China's economic system, the competitive environment for state-owned enterprises is becoming increasingly grim. Thus the task of improving their market adaptability and competitiveness becomes ever more urgent.

After more than a decade of reform and opening to the outside world, profound changes have occurred in China's economic system. A new setup has taken shape with the public ownership as the mainstay and the coexistence and common development of various economic entities such as the state-owned, collective, individual, private, and foreign-invested economies. In the allocation of resources the roles of market mechanisms have become clearer. State-owned enterprises, particularly those of large and medium-sized, have always been a leading force in the development of China's national economy and society and have made significant contributions to the flourishing and development of economic construction and reform. In general, the status and functions of these enterprises has not changed—they are still the pillar and backbone of the national economy. However, it should be noted that for several reasons the competitiveness, profit level, and speed of development of a considerable portion of state-owned enterprises are gradually losing ground to non-state-owned enterprises, most notably foreign-invested enterprises, township enterprises, and privately run enterprises. When China's national economy is being brought into line with the international economy step by step, the competitive situation faced by state-owned enterprises in the future will be even more dire. Deepening enterprise reform, liberating and developing the productive forces of the state sector through systemic innovation, and improving the all-around competitive ability of these enterprises are therefore essential.

II. Problems of Innovation Within the Chinese Enterprise System

The establishment of a modern enterprise system is a complex systematic project involving various aspects. With regards to cognition, structural inertia, and practical operation, there are bound to be a variety of difficulties; only by taking hold of these

CHAPTER I CRUX OF CHINA'S ECONOMIC STRUCTURAL REFORM

problems and solving them will breakthroughs be obtained in systemic innovation. The main problems China has encountered in its attempt to establish a new enterprise system are as follows:

1. Distribution of interests from state-owned assets

Innovation within the Chinese enterprise system (primarily within state-owned enterprises) will certainly involve ways to distribute a large chunk of state-owned assets. As to this problem, the distribution of interests is of vital importance. Improperly handled, this will retard the reform of the enterprise system. One aspect of the problem is the distribution of benefits between the central and local governments, and among local governments at all levels. Although the system is now clearly outlined—state-owned assets belong to the central government while the local governments exercise supervision—the complexity of the Chinese system lies in the fact that a significant number of enterprises are local state-owned enterprises. They are initially funded by provinces, cities, districts or counties. Were ownership to be centrally unified, local governments would be deprived of its management role. Another aspect of the problem is the distribution of benefits in stipulating property rights to state-owned assets. Normally, regardless of how large they grow, the assets of an enterprise are controlled by the original investors. But property rights to some enterprises in China are muddled, and some of them have never even received state investment, their development coming entirely from loans. If now all of these assets are defined as state property, these enterprises will be unhappy. The third aspect is the distribution of benefits in the appraisal of assets in defining property rights of state-owned assets. In the past China recognized only the concept of fixed assets, and intangible assets were generally not recorded. At present there is no scientific method of appraising intangible assets, and current methods for doing so are obsolete. Moreover, when calculating fixed assets, often the net value is obtained by simply subtracting the depreciation from the original value. There is essentially no system for periodic reappraisals based on replacement value. For a long time there has been no system for determining normal depreciation, and depreciation rates are very low. In particular, when dealing with fixed assets, debt was often not considered and there was no concept of net assets—total assets minus total debt. Therefore, appraisal of state-owned assets is very difficult, an undervaluation resulting in a drain of state-owned assets, and an overvaluation harming the interests of the enterprises.

2. Who will represent and implement the functions of ownership of state-owned assets.

Under existing circumstances there are two interrelated problems. Who will represent the ownership of state-owned assets? According to stipulations in the Regulations Concerning the Transfer of Enterprise Operational Mechanisms, the general representative is the State Council. But in view of the vast assets throughout the country and their multifarious forms of operation, implementation of these regulations would be extremely difficult. Therefore, authorized by the State Council, the administration of state-owned assets is the representative of the functions of ownership. Authorization is quite specific, but it is, in fact, difficult to implement. One reason for this is the regulation calling for separate supervision at each level which gives each locality practical authority over supervision, making it difficult for state-owned asset departments to interfere. A second reason is that many state-owned enterprises are scattered throughout central and local industries and administrative departments, which in essence possess powers of representation and comprehensive supervision. This means that unification as well as separation are equally impossible, resulting in a disorderly mix of contradiction, containment, and entanglement. The second problem is how, exactly, representation of state-owned assets will be carried out. If direct management is adopted, with no consideration for who is doing the representing, then this still amounts to an administrative way of running things, no different from the old road; if direct operation and management is not adopted, then there still exists the problem of determining the representatives of direct investors and the corresponding rights and duties of enterprises, a problem which has yet to be solved. This is the dual plight of China's state-owned asset management system.

CHAPTER I CRUX OF CHINA'S ECONOMIC STRUCTURAL REFORM

Due to the problems outlined above, departments currently in charge of managing state-owned assets are also in an awkward position: They have no power to propose reform plans, nor are they super-departmental units with plenary powers or coordinating ability. Thus, enforcing their own roles combines high cost with low effectiveness, making it difficult to bring the reality in line with the ideal.

3. The true separation of government and enterprise has not, in essence, occurred, due to the difficulty in breaking through the old framework wherein the government exercised the combined management of both assets and personal affairs.

Until now, enterprises were all under the jurisdiction of government administrators. This was accomplished mainly through government control and operation of state assets, as well as through the more practical method of appointing the heads of these enterprise from the government ranks. As long as the government appointment system continued to exist, the life line of an enterprise was simply in the hands of the government. The administrative role of entrepreneurs and the subordinate administrative relations were, in fact, a major administrative link used by the government to force enterprises into submission. Appointed administrative personnel owed their first responsibility to the administration, and the major operational personnel of enterprises were often confused, ill-qualified, and poor managers—a major factor in the phenomenon of failing production. This was at complete odds with the role of the corporate system in allowing operators the formation of mechanisms, a choice of standards, and an environment of growth. The marketization of the modern enterprise operator system is being directly coordinated in line with the modern enterprise system. Therefore, if the professionalization of enterprise management is not carried out, if a true management market is not formed, and if government and enterprises are not separated, innovation will be truly difficult to achieve within the enterprise system.

4. A lack of investors and of clear guidelines for determining responsibility within an enterprise has resulted in confusion concerning the property rights of state-owned enterprises.

The lack of investors in state-owned enterprises is made evident in many ways. For example: (1) The authority of state investment policy and allocation departments is quite large, yet they need not bear responsibility. (2) The conference on enterprises of a mixture of state financial appropriations and bank loans for use as operational assets does not make a distinction between the capital fund of an enterprise and the debt of an enterprise, and allows the creditor's bank to act as an investor, using loans to fill the investment gap. (3) The depreciation fund which should belong to the enterprise capital integrant has been taken as financial fund management, and has been turned over to financial departments and the departments in charge of the enterprise in terms of taxes. (4) Insufficient long-term collection of depreciation funds has therefore resulted in the transformation of relevant funds into false profits which are then allocated for other uses. (5) In light of the above, and for other reasons, the gap in enterprise funds is already considerable, allowing enterprise liability to replace and transform investment. In this way, enterprises that are unable to secure loans are powerless to undertake rejuvenation and remolding. Enterprises that are able to make transformations by getting loans find themselves unable to bear the burden of debt. Today they are finding it difficult to take steps toward marketization, leaving many in charge of enterprises in shock, "if an enterprise does not transform, death will come to it; if an enterprise sets out to transform, it goes in search of death." (6) Government departments have allowed banks to issue loans to enterprises using administrative guarantees backed by no assets, and in recent years government departments and banking institutions have issued bonds for enterprises which are backed by nothing—if an enterprise is unable to repay the debt, no one is held accountable.

5. Corporate property rights have not been standardized, making true independence difficult to achieve.

The core of the modern enterprise system is independent corporate property rights. This is one of the fundamental differences between the corporate system and ownership by a physical person, where the investors participate directly in handling an enterprise's assets, and where all power is concentrated in the hands of the owner. Under the planned economy, the state-owned enterprise system closely resembled that of the traditional enterprise system—the investors maintaining direct operational control over the enterprise and assuming overall authority—the only difference being that property rights reside with the government instead of with a private individual. Hence, the traditional state-owned enterprise does not adopt a true corporate system.

The problem is that we are still busily trying to mold a new corporate system out of the old model, and the standardization and independence of corporate property rights is still proving difficult to realize. This is the result of the problems cited above, which are manifested in the following manner:

a. Irrational establishment of stock rights. A general emphasis is placed on the direct establishment of "state-owned stock," with absolute control over the stock a must.

b. Incompleteness of the corporate setup. In general, a representative of the "state-owned stock" (usually someone who still retains a position as a government official) participates in the board of directors, and in practice uses their status as holder of the stock to directly control the board. The status and rights of the other directors, representing a limited portion of the stock, are hardly guaranteed.

c. Incompleteness of corporate policy-making procedures and regulations. All members of the board of directors should be equal, representing certain portions of the assets. The chairman of the board (or the stockholder) should maintain a complex relationship with the board of directors. At present however, the appointed agent of the state-owned stock tends to establish a dominant-subordinate relationship with the board of directors. Everything is thus still done according to how the government agent wants it done.

d. Decisions made by the board of directors and even by shareholder meetings must still be reported to the department in charge for "examination and approval," where they are often rashly rejected, thereby hamstringing the principles of the enterprise system.

e. The corporate status of companies lacks de facto legal protection. The corporate setup lacks even the minimal ability to defend against rights violations and interference.

f. Existing state-owned enterprises need to be transformed into companies, but they are running up against many historical difficulties.

(1) For a long time, owing to the stringent treatment given to enterprises, the injection of capital into enterprises was insufficient. This had major effects on the strength of a significant portion of enterprises, so much so that reserved financial resources were nearly non-existent.

(2) Because of the replacement of financial allocation by loans, for a considerable time the distinction between investment and creditor's rights was blurred, resulting in a disproportionately high rate of debt among enterprises and an excessive burden of principal and interest. There were even newly created "state-owned enterprises" that had no capital, only massive debts. In fact, a good portion of the debt was subsumed under capital infusion, and another portion was tucked away under reductions in employee salaries and benefits. This has become an insoluble problem in the present effort to determine property rights.

(3) Because of the lack of distinction between financial allocation and loans, policy-related loans and commercial loans have been mixed together, with many enterprises steeped in debt and no way to pay them off. This has resulted in numerous hidden "bad debts" among banks. In addition, the reform of property rights in the financial system and banks themselves has not yet begun, causing all sorts of problems for reform and business within the banking system. For example, the impact on banks of handling large amounts of credit transactions, bad debts, and bankruptcy has increased misgivings within the banking system toward enterprise reform and has led to the dampening of innovation within the enterprise system.

(4) Many state-owned enterprises have suffered losses for a quite long time. A certain proportion of these enterprises cannot meet their debts and face immanent bankruptcy. It is very difficult to deal with these enterprises economically and socially.

CHAPTER I CRUX OF CHINA'S ECONOMIC STRUCTURAL REFORM

(5) State-owned enterprises originally filled important functions in society. An "enterprise-run society" resulted in a significant portion of production capital going into semi-operational assets, greatly increasing the burden on enterprises. How these non-operational assets are to be separated from the normal operations of an enterprise is a difficult problem.

(6) State-owned enterprises have a great number of surplus employees. In addition, they have to support many retired workers and staff. All these add difficulties to the reform of state-owned enterprises, plus some social problems, such as the social insurance system that has not been set up and the long-standing "iron rice bowl" that has not been completely smashed.

To sum up, enterprise reform will not be an easy task. None of these problems are unique. On the contrary, they are ubiquitous and in urgent need of comprehensive research and solutions.

Some experts have summarized the major problems of reform by citing the following three aspects:

The first comprises three historical burdens that commonly exist in these enterprises. Foremost among these is surplus workers and staff, estimated by some to be between 20 and 30 percent, and by others to exceed 30 percent, not including retired employees which amount to another 20 percent or more. Second is the problem of debt, for which there exists no accurate measurement, though it is undoubtedly a very large amount. According to estimates uncollected debt, untransferable debt, and still operational active debt each accounts for roughly one-third of all bank loans. Of course, this is not all owed by enterprises—these figures include government debt as well. Among these, the portion that enterprises cannot pay back is generally reckoned to be around 20 to 30 percent. Out of the more than 2,000 billion yuan in loans then, this amounts to about 400 or 500 billion yuan. The third problem is that of the "enterprise-run society." This not only includes time and energy of the enterprises' leaders, but also involves the vast amount of manpower present in these enterprises. For example, the Wuhan Iron and Steel Plant originally had 120,000 employees and then laid off 70,000, or 60 percent. Anshan Iron and Steel Plant has 200,000 workers and staff and may lay off 120,000, or 60 percent. If this problem does not go away, it will be very difficult for these enterprises to be modernized.

The second concern lies in three distorted relationships, i.e., the relationships between the government and the enterprise, between laborers and the enterprise, and among the Party, the government, and workers within the enterprise (or, more simply, the relationships between the government and the enterprise, between the Party and the enterprise, between laborers and the enterprise). Not only do these relationships touch on many practical problems, they also involve theoretical ones. Why have these enterprises never taken off? Why haven't they taken effect after more than three years of transforming operational mechanisms? Basically because these three relationships have never been straightened out.

The third is that if state-owned enterprises went to deepen reform, they must surpass three major obstacles, which will probably be more difficult to solve than the previous two. First is the conceptual obstacle. How are state-owned enterprises to be viewed, and how are they to be handled? Not only are they under public ownership and control, for a long time they have been considered the highest and best part of the public ownership system. Theoretically, persisting in public ownership and a proper degree of state ownership is entirely correct. But how to practically handle this and how to find an effective method of implementation are problems which have yet to be solved.

The second obstacle is the streamlining of government agencies and the transformation of government functions. Reform of state-owned enterprises always runs into one crucial problem: The lack of distinction between government and capital, and between government and enterprises. Where enterprises are subservient to government administration, it is tantamount to the government, bureaus, and localities having direct management control over enterprises. A solution lies not only in straightening out property rights and in establishing clear and effective asset management and operational systems, but also in implementing autonomous operational rights for enterprises. To accomplish this it will be necessary to streamline specialized government organi-

CHAPTER I CRUX OF CHINA'S ECONOMIC STRUCTURAL REFORM

zations at every level and transform government functions.

The third obstacle is that of social insurance. To date, China has not established a standardized social insurance system. First of all, coverage is limited, extending only to government organs and institutions, and to some employees of collective units. This is not truly comprehensive system. Also, the cost of present social insurance system is borne by enterprises, not by society as a whole. So if employees don't receive retirement pensions, free health care, or unemployment benefits they will rely on enterprises, not on society. Therefore, no matter how poor an enterprise's performance is it will be unable to declare bankruptcy or cease production. As a result reform of the enterprise's internal management will be impossible.

How are the above three aspects, three burdens, three relationships, and three obstacles to be resolved? The best results can probably be achieved by first resolving the three obstacles, then straightening out the three relationships while simultaneously tackling the three burdens. Yet great difficulties are sure to remain. To take the reform of state-owned enterprises as a matter of the utmost importance is, of course, completely correct, which brings us to the next step, which is how to coordinate such reform.

Chapter II
Basic Thoughts on the Transformation Period for State-Owned Enterprises

I. Enlivening the State-Owned Economy as a Whole

(I) **Making clear the guiding thought for the reform of state-owned enterprises, and focusing on enlivening the state-owned economy while deepening the reform of state-owned enterprises.**

China's overall objective in reforming state-owned enterprises is to increase social productivity and strengthen the actual strength of the national economy and improve people's livelihood. The state-owned economy has always been the economic backbone of China, establishing both the structure and direction of the Chinese economy. State-owned enterprises are also the main source of revenue for the People's Republic of China. Although the last few years have brought booming development to nearly all corners of the economy—township and county enterprises, foreign-invested enterprises, and private enterprises—China's basic industries are for the most part large and medium-sized state-owned enterprises, and they hold the economic lifeblood of the country, determining in which direction the national economy will develop. The state-owned economy not only represents the development level of China's productivity, but also supports the process of reform and opening to the outside world, promotes economic development, and guarantees social stability. State-owned enterprises are the driving force that will propel China into the world market and strengthen China's competitiveness. They are the Chinese people's most important asset for achieving

CHAPTER II BASIC THOUGHTS ON THE TRANSFORMATION PERIOD

common prosperity. In the long run, whether or not the state-owned economy has the vitality to spur on development of the national economy and raise the living conditions of the people is of strategic importance. This is the reality of China's social economic development and the basis for sustained and steady growth.

China's reform timetable is in line with the socialist market economic system. Enterprises come and go while survival of the fittest is the universal law of the market economy. These competitive mechanisms build a healthy economy. Previously China had a planned economy wherein state-owned enterprises could only come into existence, never close down. These enterprises continued to receive government support regardless of their success or failure. Socio-economic resources were never distributed appropriately or used effectively which increased the burdens on the state. More than 10 years of reform have proved that "some enterprises can't die, and most aren't living well." It has also been shown that in trying to force every state-owned enterprise to succeed, those enterprises which should have "died" were dragging down the ones that were thriving. This also increased the burden on the state financial administration and the national banks. Therefore, whether viewed from the standpoint of rational economic development or the effectiveness of deepening reform, it is necessary to alter the original concept of enlivening state-owned enterprises and establish the concept that the state-owned economy isn't the same as state-owned enterprises. In further deepening the guiding thought for reform of state-owned enterprises, it will be necessary to shift attention to enlivening the national economy as a whole from rapid development of every enterprise. Through the mechanism of fiscal efficiency, economic resources should be channeled to the most effective enterprises and reorganization should achieve optimal distribution. State-owned assets should be used to carry out reorganization and transformation within the state-owned economy or an even larger sphere to move the agenda of reform forward. Superior enterprises should be able to procure at a low cost materials for production and achieve rapid development, thereby strengthening the overall strength of the state-owned economy. This is an objective requirement for obtaining qualitative advances in reform and the inevitable choice for optimizing the structure of enterprises.

(II) Raising the status and improving the roles of the state-owned economy in the national economy by bringing into full play three major advantages: distribution, organization, and structure.

China's reform experience in the past decade has shown that different systems of ownership have their own advantages within various industries. However due to China's concrete conditions, it is necessary to take the system of public ownership as the foundation and to look to the state-owned economy for guidance.

The leading roles of the state-owned economy are manifested in the following ways: First, state and collective assets occupy a dominant position in total social assets; second, the state-owned economy composed of state assets controls and influences the national economy; third, the state-owned economy plays crucial and guiding roles in improving the overall quality of the national economy; and fourth, the state-owned economy guarantees and supports the national economy by protecting social equality, promoting development, and maintaining social stability.

In bringing the leadership functions of the state-owned economy into play it is necessary to develop the superiority of state assets by improving distribution and management over those assets. We can also increase the strength of the state sector by increasing the amount of state capital. In addition, we should take advantage of the ample strength of state assets to build and develop large-scale projects which will have a great impact on the national economy. We should use stockholding methods to absorb and control non-state assets and non-state enterprises and promote organizational restructuring. In terms of structure, we should push for the optimal organization of state asset stock, reduce losses in state-owned enterprises, and ensure investment in those industries which are developing the national economy.

In accordance with China's economic development, financial

CHAPTER II BASIC THOUGHTS ON THE TRANSFORMATION PERIOD

situation and state-owned assets, it is necessary that state-owned enterprises address the following areas. First are basic public and infrastructure services, such as mail, communications and transportation, port facilities, water, and electricity. These industries are characterized by large investment, broad scope, and essential social benefits. Second are basic industries including exploration of natural resources, coal, petroleum, electricity, iron and steel, chemicals, nonferrous metals, and large-scale water conservancy projects. Third are pillar industries such as machinery, automotive, electronics, and construction. Fourth are such new- and high-tech industries as space navigation, aviation and biological engineering. Fifth are military and some special industries such as strategic and conventional weapons and currency minting. These relate to national security and therefore are necessarily monopolized and protected by the state. Sixth is one of the tertiary industries—finance. This is an important method by which the government can carry out macrocontrol and promote economic policies. Seventh are industries with obvious social benefits such as environmental protection, education and basic scientific research. These sectors are of great importance to social development.

II. Creating a Modern Enterprise System— the Basic Task for Transforming the Economic System

(I) When a modern enterprise system was proposed, this represented an important breakthrough in basic thinking about reform and a call for systemic renovation.

From 1949 until just before the start of reform and opening to the outside world, China's private economy was transformed into a public economy, which continued to develop as a fully public-owned economy. By 1978, the public-owned economy had accounted for 98 percent of China's gross domestic product (GDP) and nearly 100 percent of total industrial output value. Of that, 77.6 percent was created by industries owned by the whole people, while the remaining 22.4 percent was produced by the collective sector. Of them, urban collectively owned enterprises were organized and run in the same way as those owned by the people.

At the end of the 1970s, the policy of "taking the planned economy as the mainstay and market readjustments as supplementary" was proposed. Although mandatory planning still controlled prices, materials, investment, labor and wages, this policy did make a crack in the unitary centralization of the planned economy, by granting farmers some freedom of operation. As a result, agricultural and sideline products and more and more consumer goods became commodities, and some means of production were allowed to enter the market. Along with the founding of the market China started experiments in expanding the operational autonomy of enterprises in 1978, marked by the slogan "release right, allow profits." Beginning with adjustments in the distribution relations between the state and enterprises, various types of profit retention were implemented, bringing into play the productive initiative of enterprises, staff and workers. By the mid-1980s, the number of urban enterprises had reached over one million, with 80 million employees, and those using a profit-tax system accounted for over 80 percent of all state revenues. Enterprises in other sectors of the economy were also appearing, not only as "independent units of production" but also as "commodity producers and operators."

On October 20, 1984 the "Decision of the Central Committee of the Communist Party Concerning Reform of the Economic System" clearly stated: "China's socialist economy is a planned commodity economy," affirming the systemic status and role of a commodity economy. In order to "vigorously develop commodity production and exchange," China must "strengthen the vitality of enterprises, especially that of large-scale enterprises owned by the whole people." In addition the decision analyzed the important malpractice that led to the listlessness of the old system —"confusing ownership by the whole people with the enterprises directly operated by government organs." It proposed that according to the principle "ownership and operating rights may be

CHAPTER II BASIC THOUGHTS ON THE TRANSFORMATION PERIOD

appropriately separated," and abiding by state planning and administration, enterprises should be granted rights in production, supply and marketing, retention of capital, employment, bonuses, price, and other areas. "Enterprises should truly be turned into independent economic entities, producers, and operators of socialist commodities who operate their businesses on their own, assume sole responsibility for their profits and losses, have the ability to transform and develop themselves and become legal persons with certain rights and duties." This was the first formal Chinese government confirmation of the corporate status of enterprises (including enterprises owned by the people).

Article 41 of the General Rules of the Civil Law of the People's Republic of China, which was promulgated on July 12, 1986 and went into effect on January 1, 1987, specifies: "State-owned and collectively owned enterprises that have a certain amount of capital, articles of association, and an organizational structure and a site and are able to undertake civil responsibility should get corporate status upon the examination and approval of the department in charge." "The legal persons of state-owned enterprises shall take civil responsibility for the property under their management with approval of the state." "State-owned enterprises have operational rights over state property under their management, and this property is under the protection of law." On December 2, 1986, the Enterprise Bankruptcy Law of the People's Republic of China was adopted at the 18th Meeting of the Sixth National People's Congress, which specifies that when an enterprise "declares bankruptcy, all property under the enterprise's operation and management" should be "bankrupt property;" and the enterprise should pay off its debts according to law.

On April 13, 1988, the State-Owned Industrial Enterprise Law of the People's Republic of China was adopted at the First Meeting of the Seventh National People's Congress. As the first enterprise law in China, it clearly defines the nature, rights, and duties of state-owned enterprises in a systematic way: "State-owned enterprises are producers and operators of socialist commodities, which operate on their own, assume sole responsibility for their profits and losses, and adopt independent accounting according to law." "The enterprise's property belongs to the whole people; and the state grants enterprises power over operation and management in light of the principle of separation of ownership from operating power. Enterprises have the right to occupy, use, and handle state property with approval of the state." "Enterprises shall obtain corporate status according to law, and shall undertake civil responsibility for the state property under their operation and management with approval of the state." "The factory director is the legal representative of the enterprise."

From the Resolution made in 1984 to the promulgation of the Enterprise Law, the nature and status of enterprises as independent commodity producers and operators were made clear step by step in light of "the planned commodity economy," and "appropriate separation of ownership from operating power," thus establishing legal preparations for the reform of the enterprise system. During this period, a series of reform explorations were made. A two-step "replacement of profits by taxes" was carried out, aimed at standardizing the distribution relations between the state and enterprise with unified taxation. In addition, China reformed "price and taxation" to straighten out the price system and speed up the course of marketization, reduced the targets of the mandatory plan step by step, and lifted controls on the prices of commodities under the guiding plan and market regulation. Enterprises then tried to throw off government control and safeguard their rights under law. Especially since the end of 1986, the contracted managerial responsibility system was introduced throughout the country. Enterprises managed state-owned property under contract and guaranteed a certain amount of income to the state while retaining some income for enlarging production, raising staff and workers' income, and improving the general welfare. To meet the demands of the market, enterprises have also reformed their internal management systems, such as tailoring output to market demands and strengthening marketing, development, and information capabilities. However, during this period China spoke only of a "commodity economy" not a "market economy," did not define who would play the deciding role in allocating resources, retained administrative interferences

CHAPTER II BASIC THOUGHTS ON THE TRANSFORMATION PERIOD

which restricted market growth, and did not integrate market mechanisms with reform of the enterprise system.

Since 1990, China's economic and theoretical planners have realized that the reform of the enterprise system must take the market as its guide. In particular, during his inspection of south China, Deng Xiaoping put forward the idea that a planned economy does not equal socialism; and that a market economy does not equal capitalism. Deng's words have further emancipated people's ideology. The 14th National Congress of the Central Committee of the Communist Party of China held in October 1992 declared: The final target of the Chinese economic system is to set up a socialist market economy. It took 10 years for the Chinese people to complete the ideological transition from a planned economy to a market economy. Now the commodity market has greatly developed. Of China's total industrial output value, the products manufactured according to a mandatory plan have decreased from 80 percent in the early 1980s to less than 20 percent; and controls over the prices of about 90 percent of all agricultural and sideline products and of over 80 percent of all production have been lifted. A series of effective measures have been taken, and consequently township enterprises and foreign-invested enterprises have expanded rapidly, and the reform of state-owned enterprises now has been placed on the agenda.

On July 23, 1992 the State Council promulgated the Regulations on State-Owned Industrial Enterprises' Change of Their Operational Mechanisms, aimed at "pushing state-owned industrial enterprises to the market." In light of the basic principles of the Enterprise Law, the Regulations put forward the change of enterprise's operational mechanisms in accordance with market demands, and turn the rights granted to enterprises in the Enterprise Law into 14 operational autonomies. The promulgation of the Regulations made us work out an enterprise system according to the market economy. Within six months, 29 provinces, autonomous regions, and municipalities directly under the central government drew up the implementation rules of the Regulations one after another. Now, 14 operational autonomies prescribed in the Regulations have basically been implemented, and governmental interference in prices, mandatory plans, the enterprise business scope, the distribution system, and other aspects have been markedly reduced.

On November 30, 1992, the Ministry of Finance issued the General Rules on Enterprise Financial Affairs and the Standards of Enterprise Accounting upon approval by the State Council. The General Rules and Standards, which came into effect throughout the country on July 1, 1993, have fundamentally affected state-owned enterprises' status as the state's financial budget units, and brought the country's financial system closer to that of modern enterprises. They clearly specify: "The founding of an enterprise must have legal capital." "Capital can be divided into state, corporate, individual, and foreign capital according to the investment main bodies." "An enterprise enjoys operational power over the capital collected by the enterprise. During the period of operation, the investors may transfer their investment according to law, but may not withdraw their investment." The Standards also stipulate: "Capital is the enterprise's economic resources calculated in currency, including various properties, creditor's rights, and other rights." In essence, the state, originally the owner of state-owned enterprises, was turned into an investor; and the state enjoys the owner's rights and interests.

In 1992, China began to audit the assets of 51 enterprises. In 1993, China also audited the assets of 7,600 enterprises, of which one third were large and medium-sized enterprises. In 1994, the work of auditing assets was carried out in certain pilot cities such as Shanghai and Tianjin, and in more than 10,000 large and medium-sized enterprises. This was the largest such investigation since the initiation of reform and opening to the outside world. State-owned assets were checked, property rights were registered, and many long-standing problems affecting state-owned assets, such as insufficient compensation and "resting on their laurels," were solved. In addition, the old complete cost regulations were replaced by international manufacture cost regulations, making an enterprise's costs truly reflect production and operations. All these efforts have laid the foundation for scientifically defining property rights and correctly appraising state-owned capital funds.

While the founding of the market economic system and the completion of price reform was occurring, the development of state-owned enterprises was much slower than that of township and foreign-invested enterprises. The proportion of the output value of state-owned enterprises to total industrial output value decreased yearly, and is now less than 50 percent. One reason for this is that state-owned enterprises, as the pillar of state finance, have to pay heavy taxes. In 1992, of the country's total industrial enterprises, state-owned enterprises made up only 1.2 percent. However, their output value accounted for 48 percent of total industrial output value, and the taxes on profit paid by state-owned enterprises amounted to 63 percent of the nation's total. This situation will be alleviated with the formulation of the new tax system and the formation of an equal competition environment. Another reason is the integration of government administration with enterprise, and too much administrative interference. Consequently, enterprise autonomy over operations cannot completely be put into practice. Experience over the past 10-odd years has demonstrated that the delegating of power to state-owned enterprises cannot solve this problem fundamentally, and that it can only be solved through reform of the enterprise system.

After the 14th National Congress of the Communist Party of China (CPC), a series of surveys were made on how best to establish a macro basis for a socialist market economy. First, the First Session of the Eighth National People's Congress adopted the Amendment of the Constitution of the People's Republic of China, which changes the state-operated economy into the state-owned economy, and "state-operated enterprises" into "state-owned enterprises," correctly embodying the differences between ownership and the power to operate enterprises. Half a year later, the Third Plenary Session of the 14th National Congress of the CPC approved the Resolution of the CPC Central Committee on Certain Questions on Founding the Socialist Market Economy on November 14, 1993 which states: "The modern enterprise system with public ownership as the mainstay is the basis of the socialist market economic system. In the past decade, China has taken measures such as expanding the state-owned enterprise's autonomy over operations and reforming the operational mode, thus enlivening the enterprise's vitality and laying an initial foundation for enterprises to enter the market. To continuously deepen the reform of enterprises, we must solve the deeply rooted contradictions and make efforts to innovate the enterprise system." "Establishing the modern enterprise system is an inevitable requirement for the development of large-scale socialized production, the market economy, as well as the reform orientation of China's state-owned enterprises." "The adoption of the company system by state-owned enterprises is exploration conducive to founding the modern enterprise system. A standardized company can effectively separate investors' ownership from corporate property rights, and the functions of the government from those of the enterprise." One month later, on December 29, 1993, the Standing Committee of the Eighth National People's Congress adopted the Company Law of the People's Republic of China in order to "meet the demands for establishing the modern enterprise system, standardizing the company's organizations and behavior," and "promoting the development of the socialist market economy." On July 1, 1994, the Company Law was put into effect. On August 10, 1994, Premier Li Peng delivered the Government Work Report at the Second Session of the Eighth National People's Congress, which points out: "The state will organize a number of large and medium-sized state-owned enterprises and will make experiments on founding the modern enterprise system in accordance with the Company Law." Thus the reform of Chinese enterprises has entered a new stage, featuring changes within the state-owned enterprise's operational mechanisms and the establishment of the modern enterprise system.

(II) Establishing the modern enterprise system is the basic project in changing the economic system.

The establishment of the modern enterprise system as the objective of the reform of China's large and medium-sized enterprises is essential for establishing and perfecting the market economic system, as well as a basic project during the transition from a planned economy to a market economy. It will be of decisive significance if China can better set up the new socialist market economic system and will mark the fact that Chinese enterprises have entered a new stage.

For many years, China has taken enterprise reform as the central link in the reform of the entire urban economic system. Thanks to the efforts of many years, enterprises have strengthened their vitality, their equipment has been improved, and the production of basic industries, such as communications, energy, and basic raw and processed materials, has developed rapidly. This has also supported the development of the rural economy and the non-state-owned economy and enlivened the market generally. State-owned enterprises have made contributions to China's economic progress and reform and opening to the outside world as well. Along with the expansion of reform, the deepening of market reforms, and the rise of township enterprises and foreign-invested enterprises, the contradictions of the two economic systems that have operated simultaneously now have become prominent. In particular, some state-owned and non-state-owned enterprises as well have fallen into dire straits amid these contradictions. For instance, state-owned and non-state-owned enterprises in the textile industry have a total capability of 30 million spindles. However, only 15 to 20 million spindles are needed to meet the demands at the domestic and foreign markets. Consequently, a significant portion of state-owned textile enterprises cannot operate fully.

Because of this entire situation, many state-owned enterprises now suffer losses. In the first half of 1994, about 50 percent of all state-owned enterprises were operating at a loss. Moreover, a great amount of social capital was wasted. According to statistics, the investment in fixed assets of the state-owned economy made up 70 percent of the country's total. However, the increase in gross domestic product ensuing from this only made up 20 percent of the country's total. Therefore, further deepening the reform of state-owned enterprises and establishing the modern enterprise system have become key elements if the sustained, rapid, and stable development of the Chinese economy is to be maintained and if the socialist market economy is to be realized.

(III) The purpose of establishing the modern enterprise system is to optimize the allocation of resources.

The connotations and significance of the modern enterprise system conducive to a market economy are as follows:

First, China should establish and perfect the enterprise corporate system and the limited liability system to make state-owned enterprises become main forces in market competition rather than subordinates of government administration. In light of the Resolution of the Third Plenary Session of the 14th National Congress of the CPC and the Company Law, when state-owned enterprises are changed into companies, "the separation of ownership by investors from the enterprise's corporate property rights should first be realized," which reflected theoretical progress as compared with the phrase put forward in the Resolution of 1984—"ownership and operation rights may appropriately be separated." This separation requires the government to become the company's investor rather than its administrative organ. Like other shareholders, the government must not withdraw the capital invested in the enterprise, nor move enterprise property, nor directly interfere with the enterprise operations. "As an investor, the government will enjoy some rights, realize profits according to the amount of its investment, make important decisions, and select managers." On the other hand, "the enterprise will enjoy corporate property rights, and civil rights according to law, and undertake civil responsibilities." "The company will do business on its own by relying on corporate properties according to law, and assume sole responsibility for its profits or losses," and "will take responsibility for all debts and assets." "Shareholders will take responsibility for the company in light of their investment." The establishment of the enterprise corporate property system and the limited-liability system should cut the "umbilical cord" between enterprises and the government, and solve the problems that have stymied state-owned enterprises for a long time, such as the integration of government administration with enterprises.

Second, the enterprise should set up mutual restriction mechanisms among the board of shareholders, the board of directors, the implementation organ (managerial personnel), the board of supervisors, and intensify market restraints and improve the operational efficiency of the enterprise. In accordance with the Resolution and the Company Law, the standardized company organization will adopt the corporate management structure, through which mutual binding relations will be formed among owners, operators, and producers. Investors make investments in an enterprise and entrust the board of directors to manage their capital. The board of directors is the company's operational and decision-making organ and has the right to employ, award, and fire managerial personnel, hired to run the enterprise in line with the commodity, capital and managerial personnel markets.

The board of supervisors, composed of representatives of stockholders and representatives of staff and workers, exercises supervision over directors and managers in accordance with the company's articles of association. To select talented people to form an expert group to manage the enterprise through a management structure to the original intention of the emergence of the enterprise conforms into the market economy. This is done to ensure high efficiency and the ability to operate at a profit, thus improving the enterprise's ability to survive and compete in the market.

Third, beginning with readjusting capital composition, China should set up a mechanism for allocating state property through the market, change the unitary structure of assets in state-owned enterprises and draw social funds from all sources to improve the operational results of state assets. The resolution points out: "Standard companies" are "also conducive to raising funds and dispersing risks." In capitalist society, because of the formation of the company system, "private capital," with the concentration of the means of production and labor force as its prerequisite, directly took the form of "social capital," thus expanding the scale of production. We can make full use of the advantages of the company system to absorb social funds from all sources in various forms, such as converting the inventory of assets into stocks, issuing new shares to increase the assets, transferring and selling ownership of stock, setting up joint ventures or cooperative enterprises, to invest them in the industries that China wishes to develop to make up for the shortage of funds. The appropriate percentage of state-owned stock in a company can vary from industry to industry, depending on how widely the stock is distributed. Corporations producing special categories of goods and enterprises producing armaments should be held by the state alone. The state also should hold controlling stocks of pillar and basic industries and seek non-state investment in them to expand the role and influence of the state-owned economy. As for competitive enterprises, the state may not hold controlling stock, but only buy limited interest in these enterprises. In this way we can keep state assets within the limits of state-owned enterprises. For example, the enterprises in which the state holds an absolute controlling percentage of stocks can also be called state-owned enterprises. In short, it is essential to put state-owned stock on the market and preserve and increase their value through the modern company system under the state's macroeconomic control.

The purpose of establishing the modern enterprise system is to optimize allocation of resources. The key is to clarify property-rights relationships and promote full circulation of state-owned assets and their reasonable allocation. The current deep-seated problems faced by China's state-owned economy are characterized by an unreasonable structure and low efficiency of resource allocation resulting in losses suffered by some state-owned enterprises, the running off of a part of state-owned assets, and the waste of manpower. This situation has many causes, but the fundamental factor is that property relations in state-owned enterprises have not been straightened out, and the "big-pot" system of state-owned enterprises has not been smashed. Practice has shown that reforms which only use the distribution of interest to generate greater productivity have certain limits, although some achievements have been made. This practice cannot solve the deep-rooted economic problems. Moreover, it has created new contradictions because the vested interests of power and responsibility differ. Therefore, to establish a modern enterprise system

CHAPTER II BASIC THOUGHTS ON THE TRANSFORMATION PERIOD

it is essential to begin with a clarification of property rights, separating the government administration from enterprise management and giving leeway to the enthusiasm of the local governments and enterprises. In this way they can assume sole responsibility for profits and losses and for all civil disputes relating to ownership rights.

The current question is how to make the delineation of property rights clear. If this question is not answered it will be impossible to establish a modern enterprise system. There will be considering China's current reality and laws, there will be more obstacles and difficulties if we start by making clear who the owners of the state properties are. According to existing management principles for state-owned assets we can first make clear which level of government will act as the agent for the state-owned properties they manage, with the power to grant property rights. Of course, the reasonable allocation of resources also includes the transfer of the right to land use, the assignment of professional personnel, and the formation of all element markets. To effect such a change is in essence a profound social change, needing new ideas and a series of concrete laws to standardize the behaviors of both the government and enterprise. Now it is clear that this must be done step by step to avoid great social upheaval and reduce as many risks as possible during the course of reform.

(IV) A general paradigm for creating a new enterprise system in China may be summed up by the following formula: One central task, two major separations, three major mechanisms, and four major constructions.

The central task for establishing a modern enterprise system is to create a clearly defined legal status for enterprises as they engage in civil affairs and market competition. On the one hand enterprises must be established as a legal entity with civic powers and responsibilities according to law. On the other hand, they must be invested with independent economic interests, independent property rights, and the ability to operate independently and assume sole responsibility for profit and loss. This is the core of the restructuring of China's enterprise system. All other improvements in systems must be made around this core. In fact, as the main thread running through the entire reform process, it has become the criterion by which all assessments of progress are made. All supplementary reforms must be judged by whether or not they are most conducive to establishing enterprises as legal entities.

In order to accomplish this central task it is essential to effect two major separations: The separation of government administration from enterprise management, and the separation of social responsibilities from enterprises. The key to separating government administration from enterprise management is to find solutions to the problems of the control, administration and supervision of the government over these enterprises by straightening out property rights. To this end, the government must separate itself from the function of economic management and from its role as owner of state assets. One, the relations between the investors of the state-owned asset, and the property of the enterprise shall be adjusted by the civil law; and two, the indirect relations between the socioeconomic administrators and the administrated, i.e., the government guides enterprises by regulating and controlling the market, shall be adjusted by economic law. The key to separating society from enterprises is to free enterprises of social functions and reestablish relations between enterprises and society. Among its administrative functions, the government should perform social and economic administrative functions correctly, strengthen its functions as social administrator and at the same time vigorously foster social organizations as they take over social functions from enterprises. To strip enterprises of their social functions, we can do the following: some of them, such as housing, can be converted into commodities and put to the market; some may be included in the social security system such as old-age pensions, medical service and unemployment relief; and a part can be used for public welfare such as education and culture. Moreover, while obeying the market goal, enterprises shall safeguard the social interest according to law, such as environmental protection, assume some social responsibilities and run public

CHAPTER II BASIC THOUGHTS ON THE TRANSFORMATION PERIOD

welfare utilities.

While effecting the two major separations, it is necessary to set up three major mechanisms, namely, stimulation-restraint mechanisms within enterprise, the market, and the macroeconomy. (1) The stimulation-restraint mechanism within an enterprise refers mainly to the arrangement of risks and gains among investors, operators and staff and workers. One is to set up mechanisms for diversifying the ownership of stock and the withdrawal of investment. The number of companies wholly owned by the state should be reduced gradually and the percentages of stocks held by legal persons, staff and workers, and individuals should be increased. Also, mechanisms should be in place for managers to share the risks and gains of the enterprise so they will maintain relations of cooperation with owners. On the basis of giving top-level managers a guaranteed minimum income (managers' market competition income), they shall share certain risks and the right to claim corresponding gains. The risk income shall be permanent and dynamic, such as future stockshares and stock options. In addition, enterprises should establish restraint mechanisms for independent employment, distribution and participation by staff members and workers in decision making.

(2) The construction of the stimulation-restraint mechanism of the market will cause enterprises to become more competitive. All production elements should enter enterprises through the market so that all contracts within the enterprises (such as labor and agent contracts will be signed through the market, thus ensuring the smooth fulfillment of the contract. Market circulation of the property rights can be intensified by applying pressure to enterprises' business activities through the competitiveness of property rights. Bankruptcy mechanisms should be formed as soon as possible to hang a sharp sword over the heads of enterprises so that only the fittest survive.

(3) The construction of a mechanism for macro stimulation-restraint will create an environment for equal competition among enterprises. One way is to establish a fair, neutral and transparent framework for the functioning of the macroeconomic system, create conditions for fair taxation and equal financing, promote

the marketization of interest rates, and strictly control the scope and time limit of preferential policies. Second, macrocontrol must be exercised according to law for maintaining stability in order to create a comfortable environment for enterprises. Third, it is necessary to restrain enterprises, strengthen the management of taxation, marketize general credit and enhance social supervision and auditing of enterprises' business activities.

In the course of creating this new enterprise system four major supplementary constructions must be promoted, namely, ideological, legal, organizational, and policy construction. Ideological construction will further emancipate the mind, change traditional notions, and disseminate modern knowledge of the market economy. In this way it will become possible to learn and grasp the basic meaning of the modern enterprise system, enhance the concept of competition and the laws of market changes, broaden the field of vision, and face the world with knowledge of international practices.

Legal construction will accelerate progress toward enacting fundamental laws and strengthening and perfecting the legislative system; first of all, the law on legislative procedure should be formulated. As to some important comprehensive laws, it is necessary to set up a special legislative coordinating body to strengthen judicial work for dealing severe blows against all economic crimes and keeping economic order. By strengthening legal construction, a legal basis for the innovation of the enterprise system will be provided to standardize reform and provide legal guarantees for innovators and a good environment for the legal system.

Organizational construction will make major overhauls in the old administrative system. Some organizations will be abolished, some merged together, and others reduced in size. At the same time, new administrative organs must be set up to strengthen the general administrative, taxation, and auditing functions, vigorously develop market intermediate organizations, set up a number of industrial associations, develop market services and supervisory organs like law offices, accounting offices and asset appraising offices, and cultivate a number of organizations performing social functions.

Finally, policy construction is intended to review the large number of existing policies in accordance with demands of the enterprise system and eventually abolish those policies that run counter to reforms and those that have been outdated. Policy mechanism must be changed and new policies adopted for the formulation and implementation of laws and procedures to strengthen reform process. Information databases and forecasting models will be set up to perfect the policy feedback system.

III. Measures to Deepen the Reform of State-Owned Enterprises

(I) It is an arduous and complicated task to establish a modern enterprise system. It requires a good foundation and positive conditions to achieve major breakthroughs by experimentation and finally to reform all enterprises and make an overall change to the new system.

1. Promoting change of all operating mechanisms and establishing modern methods in all enterprises are essential. At present, we must deepen the reform in the following five aspects to secure a solid foundation and create conditions amenable to the modern enterprise system.

First, emancipating the mind and renewing those ideas closely related to innovation. One is to change the idea that state-owned enterprises are the state budgetary units. Two is to change the situation wherein state-owned enterprises are the lone organization controlling the property owned by all the people. Except for some enterprises in special industrial categories which must be wholly owned by the state, state-owned enterprises should be allowed to draw non-state funds step by step. The new idea should be fostered that enterprises with state investment holding the whole capital stock or the absolute controlling stocks can be regarded as state-owned enterprises; and a new statistical system should be designed in light of this new idea. Three is to change the traditional way in which the state exercises absolute control over state-owned enterprises and enterprises rely on the government for everything. A new viewpoint should be set up that enterprises make their own decisions, rely on themselves and undertake the risks independently in market competition. Four is to change the practice of judging the status of public ownership merely by the number of enterprises, change the tight control over the property rights of small state-owned operations and the collectives in urban areas, and establish the idea of increasing the value of assets. On the premise of ensuring the dominant position of state-owned and collective assets in the total social assets, an effective form of realizing public ownership must be found. Five is to change the idea of merely making policy readjustments in enterprises of various ownerships and types to create conditions for equal market participation among all sectors of the economy.

Second, implementing the Enterprise Law and the Regulations for Changing the Operation Mechanism of Enterprises. For most state-owned enterprises which have not become corporations, the Enterprise Law and the Regulations remain the most important legal basis for safeguarding their own rights and interests and standardizing their behavior. It is essential to increase publicity through the media on the basis of developments during the last two years to create a good environment for implementating the Regulations. All acts encroaching on the legitimate rights and interests of the enterprises should be discovered, exposed and dealt with according to law.

Third, implementing the Regulations on the Supervision and Control of the Properties of State-owned Enterprises and establishing a system of supervision and control over state-owned assets. These Regulations are a further improvement and development of the Regulations on Changing the Operation Mechanism of Enterprises. Formulated to deal with faulty controls and serious losses in state-owned assets, they stipulate that while making property rights clear, a new system of sole ownership of state-owned assets by the state, supervision by the governments at different levels, and independent operation by the enterprises shall be established. The departments and organs authorized by the State Council should be responsible for supervising state-

CHAPTER II BASIC THOUGHTS ON THE TRANSFORMATION PERIOD

owned assets according to the division of labor and should set up supervisory organs in various regions if necessary. All state-owned enterprises should introduce an asset management responsibility system and assume responsibility for preserving and increasing the value of state-owned assets. Limited stock companies, limited liability companies, Chinese-foreign joint ventures and cooperative enterprises should be standardized in accordance with the Company Law and the representatives of state property rights be clearly defined. China may exercise supervision over the state-owned assets held by companies through the investment organs or departments authorized by the state. Special attention should be paid to the problem of losing state-owned assets during the transfer of property rights ownership and reorganization. Contracting for the operation of enterprises, corporate joint operation of enterprises, operation of Chinese-foreign joint ventures and cooperative enterprises, transfer of property rights of state-owned enterprises to individuals, private enterprises and investors from outside China must obey the Regulations on the Supervision and Control of the Properties of State-Owned Enterprises.

Fourth, reforming the enterprise management system and strengthening internal management. State-owned enterprises should, first of all, adhere to and improve the factory director (manager) responsibility system and ensure that factory directors (managers) exercise their rights and responsibilities according to law. It is necessary to introduce the competition mechanism, test and choose outstanding persons as directors (managers) of the enterprises, establish a system of verifying qualifications of business managers by achievement examination and auditing, and try out the annual salary system for business managers to create conditions for the gradual formation of a reserve of managerial personnel.

Fifth, accelerating adjustment of the organizational structure of enterprises. It is necessary to make an analysis of state-owned enterprises to determine the industries that must be supported, developed, gradually adjusted or eliminated. The structure of state-owned assets must also be adjusted in a planned way. China should establish a number of large enterprise groups (transregional and transtrade) with large and medium-sized state-owned enterprises as the mainstay and property rights as links. Experiments in operations of state-owned assets in a small number of large groups can include the setting up of import and export corporations and financial companies to become backbone forces in market competition at home and abroad. China should speed up reform of the property rights of small state-owned enterprises and collective enterprises in rural areas and form them into contracted operations, shifting them to a partnership system of stock-sharing, or selling them to collectives or individuals. The income from the sale of enterprises and the ownership of stock should be used specially for structural adjustment to replenish the funds of backbone enterprises, in conformity with the state's industrial policy. A small number of enterprises which are unable to repay their debts and conform to the conditions for bankruptcy should declare bankrupt according to the procedures stipulated in the Bankruptcy Law.

2. Making major breakthroughs through experimentation. At present, experimentation is being made on establishing a modern enterprise system in some enterprises and on supplementary reforms in some cities. We must experiment simultaneously both inside and outside enterprises and combine changing mechanism with increasing strength in an effort to achieve breakthroughs in these major and difficult problems.

First, a breakthrough should be achieved in making clear the property rights. The organs or departments authorized by the government should be defined. They are the investment main bodies of state-owned assets. The organs authorized by the state can take the form of state investment cooperations, state holding companies, state-owned assets companies or qualified state-owned group corporations. These corporations (or companies) must be wholly owned by the state, holding state-owned stock at different or overlapping levels. If it is difficult to determine the state-owned investment body for a certain experimental enterprise, the government can name a specific department and set up an independent body within that department to control the state-owned stock. But such a body would not be allowed to exercise the administrative function of the government.

Second, a breakthrough must be made to change the functions of the government. The functions of the government can be divided into three parts: Its administrative functions can relatively concentrated or merged into the general economic administrative department; its industrial administrative functions can be gradually transferred to industrial associations; and its functions for controlling state-owned assets may be gradually shifted to investment corporations or state-owned assets companies.

Third, there must be a breakthrough in establishing internal checks and balances mechanisms. The experimental enterprises should strictly observe the Company Law and the company's articles of association and choose the chairman and vice-chairmen of the board according to legal procedure. The managers shall be appointed or removed by the board of directors, not directly by the government administrative organs or the board of investors. The board of supervisors shall be composed of representatives of the investors and an appropriate proportion of representatives from the staff and workers. Directors, managers, and chief of the financial department shall not be supervisors. Government functionaries shall not be concurrently directors, managers or supervisors. The salaries of the senior managerial staff, including the manager, shall be decided by the board of directors, and salaries of the directors and supervisors shall be decided by the investors. In short, it is necessary to set up an internal mechanism for mutual stimulation and restrictions according to law.

Fourth, a breakthrough must also be achieved for installing bankruptcy mechanisms. China should begin with bankruptcy for enterprises which have suffered losses over a long period of years and are unable to satisfy their debts, and, through this bankruptcy, implement the principle of state-owned enterprises assuming sole responsibility for their profits and losses while the state assumes limited responsibility. At the same time, China will promote the trade and circulation of state-owned assets through the market and stimulate the establishment of a social security system.

Fifth, the structure of assets and liabilities of enterprises must also be adjusted. On the basis of asset inventories, assets can be checked against liability statements submitted by the corporations, registered capital should reach the legal minimum limit and be the actual capital, and any gap should be filled by investors. Moreover, the existing urban assets must be adjusted in a planned way, step by step, and the income from the sale of part of the state-owned assets used as the source of new capital. It is also necessary to search for effective means of changing the creditor's rights into the ownership of stock. The structure of assets and liabilities of state-owned enterprises should be readjusted through various channels so that those needing support and development can gradually shake off the heavy burden of debt and begin a positive growth cycle.

Sixth, it is also essential to make a breakthrough in establishing a social security system by taking full advantage of the cities to unify social insurance organizations and gradually raise the extent of coverage. China should make efforts to change the sole channel (mainly enterprises) for covering the insurance funds, expand the sources of these funds and find a way to convert part of the state-owned assets to finance pensions for retired staff and workers. A preferential tax policy should be offered to service enterprises run mainly by surplus staff and workers (their proportion now exceeds 60 percent) to increase job opportunities. Public welfare facilities run by the enterprises may be gradually shifted to local communities and large cities.

3. Turning state-owned enterprises into modern enterprises according to law, by categories and in groups. Making innovations in the state-owned enterprise system is an extremely arduous and complicated task. It must be done according to law and in a standard manner. In order to ensure the smooth implementation of the Company Law, China is now drafting Interim Measures of the State Council for Reorganizing State-Owned Enterprises into Companies and the Circular of the State Council on Standardization of Existing Companies in Accordance with the Company Law. These two documents are intended to solve the problem of shifting existing state-owned enterprises to a modern enterprise system in accordance with the law and presents methods for

standardizing existing companies, already named limited liability and limited stock liability companies.

In accordance with these two documents, state-owned enterprises shall be reorganized into companies according to the aforementioned categories and groups. A small number of enterprises producing specialized goods, along with public utilities, can be reorganized into companies wholly owned by the state. The competitive enterprises in other industries and trades should be reorganized mostly into limited liability companies, and some into limited stock liability companies, but the state should hold the controlling stock of key enterprises in the pillar and basic industries. National corporations can be reorganized step by step into holding companies and the collective enterprises in cities and towns can be shifted to a partnership system in the form of stock sharing. In all cases it will be important to guard against precipitous action.

(II) In light of the difficult problems in the reform and development, China should combine the resolution of the difficulties and historical tasks of state-owned enterprises with the innovation of the state-owned enterprise system, and make bold breakthroughs so as to achieve substantial progress in the experiments of the modern enterprise system.

Establishing a modern enterprise system within state-owned enterprises presents a variety of problems. These cannot be solved by one single action alone. We should tackle one or two difficult problems of innovation and attempt breakthroughs in those specific areas. In the light of recent practice, there are two things we can do to solve our difficulties and promote innovation in the state-owned enterprise system.

1. Beginning with solving the problem of high debt, China will actively seek ways of improving internal management and bringing about a positive growth cycle by restructuring liabilities.

China should introduce social medium intermediate to reorganize the liabilities of state-owned enterprises and combine the solution of the liabilities of state-owned enterprises with the innovation of the state-owned enterprise system. Credit rights can be bought from the banks through social intermediate organizations to allow intermediate organizations to change the rights of enterprises creditors to stock ownership or to investment in the enterprises to return part of the bank loans. This will help lighten the debt burden of state-owned enterprises and make the assets-liabilities ratio more reasonable. It will also diversify the investors of state-owned enterprises and promote changes in the way state-owned enterprises do business. In the course of reorganizing liabilities, the enterprises can also reorganize management with the help of specialized organs to fundamentally improve the quality of their assets and management.

2. China should establish the entrusting procedures and the agent system for state-owned property rights as soon as possible to push forward the reform of the management system for state-owned properties and promote the separation of government administration from enterprise management.

In experimenting with a modern enterprise system within state-owned enterprises, it is first necessary to make clear the property rights of state-owned assets in state-owned enterprises and solve the problems of investing in state-owned assets and the operation of state-owned capital in the market economy. At present, it is difficult to further improve the management and operation of state-owned assets in a short time, but it is desirable to begin to make clear state-owned assets investment main bodies and through the authorization by the government, entrust the investment main bodies with exercising the functions of investors and gradually establish the entrustment procedures and agent system. Entrusted by the government, state-owned asset investment main bodies exercise the rights of investors, are charged with the market operation of state-owned capital, and are held responsible to the state for preserving and increasing the value of state-owned assets. State-owned asset investment main bodies shall be reorganized by relying on large state-owned investment companies, state-owned holding companies, state-owned group corporations or the existing administrative departments for the

CHAPTER II BASIC THOUGHT ON THE TRANSFORMATION PERIOD

enterprises. They shall be reorganized into corporations with exclusive state funds according to law so that state-owned asset investment main bodies shall become enterprise legal entities.

Chapter III
Reform of the Property Rights System: A Breakthrough in the Reform of State-Owned Enterprises

I. Making Clear Property Relations for the Transition to a Modern Enterprise System

(I) By analyzing the experience gained and lessons learned during the reform of the past decade-plus, we can conclude that if property rights relations are not changed the problems within the state-owned economy cannot be solved and the operation mechanisms of state-owned enterprises cannot be truly changed.

The reform of the state-owned economy began in the early 1980s. In the first stage reform gave some decision-making power to enterprises, allowed them to keep a part of their profit, and removed restrictions on the price of commodities. Because the highly centralized management system was gradually relaxed and enterprises gained certain autonomy over their business operations, they began to take market demands into consideration and market mechanisms were introduced to the state-owned economy. However, as reform has stalled at the operational level and has not yet touched upon deeper problems, especially the slow reform of the property rights system, state-owned enterprises have remained within the framework of the traditional system. This is manifested in the following ways:

1. As the enterprises still do not have sufficient independent decision-making power, their freedom of operation has been restrained, and they have been slowed and are unable to make

CHAPTER III REFORM OF THE PROPERTY RIGHTS SYSTEM

quick responses to market demands.

2. Stimulation mechanisms are insufficient. As the distribution relations between the state and enterprises have not yet been straightened out, and the distribution of income between enterprises and their staff and workers has yet to be perfected, enterprises lack effective stimulation mechanisms.

3. Enterprises are without a corporate property structure. The laws state only that operation rights belong to enterprises, but they do not declare that the enterprises possess the corporate property at their disposal. In the operation of China's macroeconomy the properties operated by enterprises and direct state properties have not been differentiated. Therefore, enterprises not only are without money to make independent decisions, they also lack the power to adjust their property structure. This being the case, enterprises find it impossible to hold themselves responsible for the operation of their assets or for preserving and increasing the value of the state-owned assets.

4. Restrictive mechanisms are insufficient. The direct state property system inevitably leaves the state responsible for enterprise losses as the enterprises themselves remain responsible for profits, but not for losses. Soft budget restrictions bring no pressure to bear on enterprises to go all out and improve and adjust their business operation. As a result, most enterprises are hungry for investment and excessive consumption, an expression of their short-sighted behavior.

5. State ownership, because of the "property rights in name only," has not been effectively and fully exercised and the owner has not shown concern for and support of assets nor exercised guidance and control over major enterprise activities, especially the balancing of short-term behavior.

The defect in China's current enterprise property rights structure lies in the fact that enterprises do not adapt themselves to the market. As a result, market mechanisms in the state-owned economy are not complete, the current mechanisms are ineffective, and the market regulatory role is weak. This is manifested by the following:

1. Competitiveness in the market is weak. Market competi-

tion, whether in price, quality or service, is based on the main bodies' rights, interests, and responsibilities. The clear delineation of and guarantees for interest relations are the pre-requisites for positive competitive behavior. Only when state-owned enterprises are changed into the main bodies of interest, can they form a competitive consciousness and go all out to participate in market competition. Most Chinese enterprises at present, because of defects in the structure of property rights, can only take part in market competition to a limited degree: (1) Enterprises do not readjust their prices on their own initiative in a timely manner to reflect market demands. (2) They also do not make efforts to readjust their product mix, nor produce high-quality new products from time to time to make them more marketable. (3) They often do not go all out to promote their products, nor improve methods of promotion and after-sale services. (4) They do not spare no effort to improve their skills and technological processes, nor to improve their business operations and cut costs so as to fundamentally increase their competitive power. (5) Enterprises are not making adjustments to the structure of their property rights, optimizing existing assets, or adjusting their organizational structure to raise the enterprise's productive capacity as a whole. In short, lacking full competitive consciousness is the common feature of behavior within state-owned enterprises at present. The competition mechanism is the internal lever for the market mechanisms. The interrelated role of price and demand is exactly determined by the competition mechanism. When the force of competition is insufficient, the market mechanism is weakened.

2. Price mechanisms are sluggish. Specifically speaking, the interrelated role of price and demand is not yet sufficiently established. When the supply of commodities is greater than the demand and stocks greatly increase, prices are not adjusted in a good timely way. This is the inevitable outcome of weak competitiveness.

3. The market mechanism role in adjusting the structure is weak. Due to lack of a loss mechanism in enterprises, the negative change of the prices is powerless. Even if the commodities are unmarketable and defective, their prices cannot be lowered, thus

demonstrating this sluggish price mechanism. As a result, the processing industries are overdeveloped while urgently needed basic industries remain underdeveloped. The outdated and all-embracing organizational setup of industrial enterprises cannot be changed, and enterprises whose assets are insufficient to offset their debt for years and which have no ability to survive competition exist in large numbers. At the same time, large numbers of redundant staff and workers useless to the enterprises cannot be fired or transferred.

4. Enterprises are too slow reacting to the market. Traditional state-owned enterprises do not react to the market because of the direct state-owned assets structure and sole state responsibility for profit and loss. The reformed enterprises, however, motivated by gains, react to positive changes in market prices, and market mechanisms have forced those enterprises with quick-selling products and good profits to rapidly expand production. However, the mechanism for negative price changes remains weak, especially in enterprises responsible only for profit, but not for losses. Even when the market is declining, and prices drop before an anticipation of losses, these enterprises often have no sense that they may be in trouble. They are not, therefore, eager to adjust their structure or perfect their management. As marketization of the economy develops traditional support for these enterprises weakens and competition becomes more and more fierce, their slow reaction to the market puts them in a difficult position. One third of all state-owned enterprises are losing money, another one third suffer hidden losses, while the remaining one third have shown profit. This is directly related to slow reaction to the market and insufficient motivation toward self-improvement.

Along with the development of urban reform, the market mechanism is gradually being introduced to the state-owned economy and the role of price formation in competition is growing. This role is also rising in the allocation of resources. However, it must be remembered that the state-owned economy, still in the initial stages of marketization, is characterized by defective and incomplete market mechanism, ineffective price mechanisms and weak market regulation and control.

The problem of losses suffered by Chinese state-owned enterprises has now come to the people's attention. According to official statistics reported in August 1994, 46.4 percent of all state-owned enterprises are operating at a loss. This does not include those enterprises which have profits on their books, but still more unpaid debt—this is called hidden losses. People often believe this is due to weakening efficiency, declining production and waste. In fact, the current problem of losses is mainly caused by the system under which capital rights are weakened in distribution.

An increase of productivity means a rise in net output, and profit is only part of the net output (net output value). The two other parts of net output are "wage cost" and "management cost." Research has shown that since the beginning of reform the fastest growth on the books of state-owned enterprises are in the areas of expenditures for wages and the cost of management. Expenditures on wage include bonuses and general welfare. If all types of material benefits given to staff and workers are counted as "material consumption cost," the growth of wage expenditures has been even more rapid. This is exactly what is meant by the "erosion of profit by wages." In the state's view, this is the "distribution of income inclining toward individuals." This analysis may not be true for a few enterprises, but so far as the entire state-owned economy is concerned the above conclusion can be verified by data and experience. In short, state-owned enterprises now produce more goods with the same amount of resources, but their profits are less and what they give to the owner of capital, namely the state, is also less. This results from the weakening of capital rights in the chain of distribution. Increased enterprise losses are not in essence a problem of "poor management" and "low productivity," but rather a problem of increasing costs and the practice of "reporting less profit." Therefore, behind the problem of reported losses lies, in essence, the problem of property rights relations and the problem of encroachment upon the owners' right to profit. In fact, the concept of profit rate is, first of all, a concept of property rights. The Western theory of

CHAPTER III REFORM OF THE PROPERTY RIGHTS SYSTEM

"entrusting—trustee" for analyzing enterprise behavior developed in a private economy is preconditioned by the existence of full motivation and trustees with no need for supervision. For the state-owned economy, the first question is the lack of an "ultimate trustee" with true motivation and interest in the efficient management of assets.

The weakening of capital rights and the lowering of profit rates inevitably lead to instability of the macroeconomy and the lack of dynamic efficiency throughout the entire economy. To change this state of affairs and to stop the losses of state-owned enterprises it is essential to rectify "property rights relations" and reestablish effective capital rights to balance the interests of managers and workers. In this way certain people in an enterprise will be truly concerned about the distribution of its income and effectively supervise the enterprise's behavior. The outstanding problem in China's state-owned economic sector since economic reform began has been the question of who supervises and controls capital interest and who represents capital to achieve profit for income distribution. The abstract concept that everyone is a "master" but no one is responsible to the state as owner of the capital has been proved unsuccessful by the fact that enterprise losses continued to grow.

(II) To establish a modern enterprise system, China must reform the current property rights system and establish the corporate property system so that property rights will truly be owned by the clearly defined corporation.

1. Property rights shall be held by legal entities.

In view of the fundamental defect in traditional state-owned enterprises, it is essential at present to readjust and reorganize the traditional structure, provide the enterprises with legal property rights, and at the same time change the direct ownership by the state into the ultimate ownership. We call this reform of state-owned property rights "the holding of property rights by the legal entities."

(1) With the capacity of the legal person granted by law, an

enterprise, like an individual, can carry out independent production and business activities, independently sign contracts with other enterprises and business managers, and are entitled to all civil rights and must assume civil responsibilities.

(2) The assets which the state invests in an enterprise, namely the capital funds, are granted to the enterprise in the form of "corporate property" through legal authorization, and the enterprise then enjoys the right to control, benefit from and dispose of assets according to law. This is, in essence, implementation of a system of entrusted property management under which the owners of the property give up the right of direct control. They do not directly interfere with the day-to-day business activities of the enterprise and they cannot withdraw their property shares from the enterprise.

(3) Enterprises, relying on their legal property, make independent business decisions and benefit from the operations of said property. For example, the profit of the enterprise, apart from being the income of the owner's property, shall be retained as enterprise accumulation for self development and entitlement for all staff members and workers as benefits.

(4) Enterprises assume sole responsibility for profit and loss with the corporate property. The corporate property of the enterprise is independently controlled by the enterprise and is used for development, assuming risks, and payment of debt in case of bankruptcy.

(5) Establishing a new form of owner's rights, interests and responsibility. The owner of the property under the corporate system, in his capacity as investor, grants direct property controlling rights to the enterprises and the state no longer directly organizes business and production. However, this is only a change in the form of property control and realizing property rights, and by no means abandons the ownership of the main body. The state still a. holds supreme and ultimate ownership by law; b. holds core ownership in the modern economy—the right to benefit from the property, namely to draw share interest and dividends; c. holds the right to choose enterprise managers and take part in making and controlling the major policies of business operations,

CHAPTER III REFORM OF THE PROPERTY RIGHTS SYSTEM

such as investment, capital accumulation, issuing new stocks and bonds, and dividend distribution policy; and d. the state is also involved in the limited liability of the limited shares of investments. This means an end to the system of eating from the big cauldron of state-owned capital funds under which the state assumed unlimited liability for enterprises.

(6) China needs to set up the enterprise organizations for effective safeguarding ownership, the rights of business management, and the mechanisms for policy making. The corporate property system which separates ownership from the rights of business management should be established on the basis of entrusting and authorizing the managers and at the same time controlling and supervising them. Only through entrusting and authorization is it possible to ensure the rights of business management, and only through control and supervision can we avoid short-sighted behavior by enterprise managers, and "superficial profit but actual loss," and prevent the loss of state property. Therefore, it is necessary to establish an appropriate form of enterprise organization, that is, the corporate system. The modern stock company needs to establish the board of directors, hold stockholders' meetings, appoint managers, and set up decision-making mechanisms. The meeting of the stockholders is the supreme forum of power for the owners, the board of directors is the trustee for the management of the property, and the general manager is responsible for organization and management of the enterprise. Through the appropriate division of powers and functions among these three entities with each fulfilling its own duty and exercising mutual checks and balances, they exercise the entrusted management by effectively ensuring the right of ownership, thus making corporate business management independent. Moreover, the board of supervisors exercises supervision over the activities of the meeting of the stockholders, the board of directors, and the manager. This is an indispensable requirement for ensuring the healthy operation of a complicated organization.

(7) The integration of the enterprise's corporate property rights. To strengthen the market mechanisms, the country employing the market economy has a task of making their state-

owned and cooperative enterprises integrate their property rights, intensify their dominant positions at the market and enhance their competitiveness. To adapt to the needs of the market economy, China's state-owned enterprises should not only implement the Enterprise Law and the Regulations, but also further expand their operation power, such as the power over investment, and production equipment.

2. Property rights shall be clearly defined.

An effective corporate system is pre-conditioned by a clear definition of property rights, including: a. the defining of the main bodies. This calls for defining the roles of owners, managers and creditors of the enterprises; b. the defining of the dominant property rights, and the clear division of property rights, interests and responsibilities. In this way, an enterprise will operate in good order and will be full of vitality.

The clear division and definition of ownership and management right is an important starting point and condition for establishing the corporate property system. For this purpose, it is first of all necessary to distinguish enterprise assets in the form of value from enterprise real property. It is then necessary to define property rights of main bodies by dividing these two kinds of property rights. Under the cooperate property system property rights of the owners are mainly manifested in the form of value, namely the right to invest. On the other hand, the concrete form of value of capital lies in such fixed assets as machinery and equipment, finished products, liquid assets, raw and processed materials, cash and accounts receivable, and intangible assets such as business credibility. The rights of day-to-day operation and control belong to the corporate entity.

It is evident that the establishment of corporate property rights is another important adjustment in the traditional structure of property rights under which the state directly controls both the value form of property and the concrete and material form of enterprise property. The right to control the concrete form of property which originally belongs to the owner, then becomes the right of the managers. Therefore, when instituting the modern enterprise system, it first requires that people change

CHAPTER III REFORM OF THE PROPERTY RIGHTS SYSTEM

their traditional notion of regarding the owner's rights as the right to control both the value of the property and the actual property itself. This traditional notion is deeply rooted in the minds of many people, becoming more and more an obstacle to reforms.

The distinction between ownership and management right is the important concept for redefining property rights. Therefore, it is necessary to have definite and detailed rules stating exactly who controls and benefits from which aspect of the enterprises.

In short, the clear and concrete demarcation between ownership and management right is the basic condition for founding the modern corporate system at present. The limits of ownership, management right, and creditor's rights should be made clear in accordance with laws and regulations, and their contents should be definite. Only in this way it is possible to ensure the state's ownership, strengthen the enterprise's management right, and safeguard the debtor's property rights. If there is no specific demarcation, not only it is difficult for the framework of property separation of ownership and corporate rights to operate, but conflicts will arise between ownership and management right. As a result, if the right of management will be restricted, the state's ownership be weakened, and the debtor's property rights be infringed upon.

3. The property right system shall be established by law.

Property rights in a modern society are safeguarded and ensured by law. Only with the aid of mandatory laws and the mechanisms for enforcing those laws, is it possible to standardize business behaviors and form a stable order of property ownership. In order to facilitate the establishment of the enterprise's corporate system it is first essential to speed up the legislative process. The Company Law has already been enacted. For now, it is necessary to accelerate the formulation of economic, civil, commercial and social laws. It is essential to establish a complete legal system which can effectively standardize the behavior of owners and managers and all parties to commercial activities—creditors, debtors, renters and leasees, and administrators.

Laws regarding relations between the ownership and management of the enterprise's property must be strictly enforced. For those enterprises which utilize the corporate system, they must be authorized to manage state-owned assets according to law, and it must be made public that state-owned assets are the enterprise's corporate property and the right to control the assets belongs to the corporation and that the administrative organs of the government have no right to transfer properties from one enterprise to another or ask for any part of gains or profits. If this should occur, it would constitute a violation of the law and the enterprise would have the right to file suit with judicial organs who would then hear the case and affix responsibility for any offense. On the other hand, it is essential to establish legal mechanism to safeguard the owner's rights, such as the right to profit from state-owned property—the interest on the state-owned shares and dividends. This will safeguard the investor's major policy-making powers and the legal mechanism to ensure the preservation and increase of the value of state-owned property while halting illegal losses. It is now essential to take legal sanctions against the many erosions of state-owned assets in the course of introducing the corporate and stock systems. These activities include the illegal transfer of state-owned assets to collective property or into the hands of private individuals, underestimating the value of state-owned assets, and infringing on the rights and interests of the state. Moreover, when the securities market, which was established not long ago, has begun to grow and become a very "hot" item, it is essential to accelerate legislation and adopt rigorous legal means to standardize the stock market and punish unlawful manipulating, the purchasing of stock in violation of the rules, and the holding of controlling stock interests by other corporations in violation of regulations. This is also an essential condition for establishing an open, fair and impartial market in order to safeguard the property rights of investors and the enterprise corporate property right. In short, the key to whether or not the corporate system can be truly established lies in the perfection and strengthening of the law and the legalization of property rights and economic mechanisms. Therefore, the acceleration of economic legislation and law enforcement, and the vigorous institution of a legal system to monitor economic behavior have

CHAPTER III REFORM OF THE PROPERTY RIGHTS SYSTEM

become prerequisites for pushing reforms forward.

4. Property rights shall be mobile.

The mobility of property rights is intrinsic to the corporate system and is also another important goal for the reform of the property right system of state-owned enterprises. Under the traditional planned economy, the holder of enterprise property owned by the people was the state, with the government making planned and monopolistic allocations of assets to enterprises, and not permitting them to transfer their fixed assets on their own initiative. As a result of the administrative divisions among different ministries and regions, the state-owned assets were like stagnant water, permanently immobile. This was a very rigid system for the allocation of production materials and resources and led to unreasonable allocation and inadequate use of state-owned assets. This stagnation and idleness of large assets kept great amounts of capital from being fully utilized. A major goal in establishing the corporate property system is to fundamentally change this immobility of state-owned enterprise assets.

Under the corporate property system, the enterprise's legal persons shall hold property rights, including the right to dispose of and transfer their property, and companies and enterprises can, by exercising their right of transfer, sell their idle machinery and equipment or transfer part of their patent and trademark rights. Companies or enterprises may also purchase or annex other factories and enterprises and buy invention rights. Moreover, this new system will open the way for the emergence of the integration of enterprises. In short, the corporate property makes it possible for enterprises to achieve the optimum combination of concrete property management and effective utilization of assets. It will also allow enterprises to operate their business independently, assume sole responsibility for profit and loss, and gives them the internal motive force to pursue the effective handling of their assets. Corporate property turns enterprises into the true holder of property rights, thus forming the micro foundation for mobile property rights. The market growth and the formation of the property rights market have given birth to a mechanism for the transfer of property rights among enterprises, which is the prerequisite for modern corporate enterprises' ability to make self-adjustments of their assets and adapt to the market. This is also the principal requisite for modern companies' ability to survive and develop amid fierce competition.

The reform aimed at establishing the corporate property system must be combined with the mobility of property rights. This is especially true for traditional enterprises in China which are all-embracing in the structure of organization and have become an obstacle to the introduction of the stockholding system. Therefore, the smooth progress in the reform of the enterprise corporate property system calls for the mobility of property rights.

5. Property rights shall be diversified.

The diversification of property rights means a diversity in the main bodies of the property. The characteristic of the traditional structure of property for state-owned enterprises is single state ownership, while the main characteristic of the corporate system is the diversified main bodies. Except for the companies with exclusive capital, the legal persons of companies all adopt the property structure of the combination of many investors. The diversification of the main bodies of property rights is the main requisite for the successful operation of corporate enterprises. Because there are many investors it is possible to direct the agents of the owners to make fair and strict choices of managers and to exercise effective supervision over them. To make a true separation of the functions of the government from those of enterprises, state-owned enterprises should secure the independent management of enterprises with owners exercising effective control and supervision. During the transition from enterprises to companies, except for certain specially designated enterprises which will remain to be enterprises with exclusive capital, most enterprises should introduce diversified shareholders or the public shareholders. The structure of diversified property rights includes stocks held by many state-owned legal persons, and the mixed ownership of stock by the state, collectives, individuals and overseas investors. This will change the traditional unitary structure of state-owned property. In addition, China should actively create condi-

CHAPTER III REFORM OF THE PROPERTY RIGHTS SYSTEM

tions and adopt measures allowing corporate stock to come to the market while also putting state-owned stock into market circulation. Only in this way it is possible to form the mechanisms for effectively safeguarding and perfecting diversified stock ownership.

The diversification of main bodies also means the merging and combining of enterprises, indispensable for the combination of capital, optimization of enterprise structure, and expansion of enterprises' scale of production to develop increased production capacity and strengthen market competitiveness.

It can thus be seen that founding the enterprise's corporate property must be combined with diversified main bodies of property rights so that enterprises not only have their property at their disposal, but corporate properties with adequate and ever growing capital funds. At the same time, it is an organization which can operate independently in accordance with regulations.

II. What Are the Independent Property Rights of the Enterprise's Legal Person?

(I) The concept of property rights has been introduced from the West. It is generally held that these rights include the right to use the economic resources of society, and the right to use profit and transfer such property rights.

The theory of property rights was first advanced by an American-born British Ronald Coase, winner of the 1991 Nobel Prize for Economics. When his book *Nature of an Enterprise* was firstly published in 1937, it did not catch the attention of the academic circles. It was not until the 1960s, the book began to be quoted as a classic. Since then, the property right economists represented by R. Coase have become an important pillar of the New System school in the United States and he himself also became the founder of the New System school. His main academic contribution lies in discovering and revealing the significance of the cost of transactions and the property rights to the economic system structure and its mode of operation and the role it plays in the allocation of the social resources and the economic growth. This is an important breakthrough in the research in the field of the structural change of the system and the system innovation.

The definitions expressed about the property rights by the people who believe in R. Coase's theory are not all the same. However, there is one generally acknowledged belief that property right is a right granted by a society for the use of economic resources. In a general sense, this integral property right expresses itself in a group of rights called "the bunch of rights": The right to use certain resources, the right to profit from the use of such resources, and the right to transfer the use of resources and profit from them within the limits permitted by law. It is necessary to stress that superficially property rights seem to describe the relations between man and an object, but in essence it reveals the mutually recognized relations of behavior among people arising from the existence of the object and its uses. A given property rights system determines the standards for the behavior of every man to that object and every man must observe the mutual relations between himself and others.

The divisibility of property rights is another important feature. Property rights can be classified primarily as the right to use, the right to profit, and the right to transfer. If it is further differentiated, each right can be specifically subdivided, thus forming a varied structure of property rights. It may thus be inferred that another feature of property rights is that they must be defined, and therefore limited and restricted. This is because the divisibility of property rights means that various rights coexist within the same structure and that each right can only be exercised within those specified limits, and beyond those limits are restricted by other rights.

When property rights remain undivided and are concentrated together in a main body, the property rights in this condition equal ownership as generally understood. So we understand that ownership is a property right in a given form. The transfer of ownership includes the permanent transfer of all rights that constitute property rights. Moreover, there is another situation in which, under the premise of unchanging ownership, property

CHAPTER III REFORM OF THE PROPERTY RIGHTS SYSTEM

rights can be shifted from one ownership main body to another, and through the division and demarcation of property rights, a new and different property rights structure will be formed. This is of very important practical significance in the discussion of the public property rights system and especially for reform of the state-owned property rights system.

In economic life to the present there has been three typical property rights systems: Private property rights, common property rights and state-owned property rights. Private property rights refer to the right to use resources by a given person enjoying exclusive right to use the property, realize a profit, and transfer the property freely. Common property rights mean that every member of the community is entitled to these rights and others are excluded from interfering with the exercise thereof by the members of the community. State-owned property rights theoretically refer to the possession of these rights by the state.

It is necessary to point out that in the eyes of Western economists private property rights are the ones most clearly defined and are most efficient only under conditions of the right to private property. Although the social system in China dictates against taking the road of making all property private, the method of analysis employed by property rights economists elsewhere has provided us with a large field for studying the impact of the different structures of property rights on an economy where non-private property rights prevail. On the one hand, under the state-owned property rights system, the property rights are separated from ownership (or on the premise of not changing the state ownership, property rights are shifted to another main body through a certain procedure), so that the new property rights main body assumes the responsibility for the preservation and increase of the value of state-owned assets. On the other hand, through the transfer or diversification of ownership, a new property rights main body will be set up to improve economic efficiency and promote economic growth.

Property rights have the following characteristics:

1. The rights enjoyed by the investors;
2. The rights arising from investments (capital invested into

enterprises);

3. Property rights for the capital invested in enterprises;
4. The rights established according to law and protected by law;
5. Rights and interests embodied in the capital that can be divided, combined, and transferred;
6. A right which can influence the enterprise's corporate property rights according to law; and
7. A right to profit from investment.

As investors make investments with their own assets, they are the capital owners as well as investors of enterprises. The investors authorized by the state are the organs which use state-owned assets to make investments. Therefore, the owners of the state-owned capital are not the investors of enterprises. The ownership of state-owned capital and the property rights of the investors embodied by the invested state capital can be separated, namely, the state enjoys the right to own the state capital while the investment organs authorized by the state enjoys the investor's property rights embodied by the state investments. In tens of thousands of state-owned enterprises, the ownership of state-owned capital is concentrated and unified while the enterprise's property rights are diversified.

The separation of the ownership and property right of state-owned assets and the establishment of many main bodies of property rights with relative interests within the state-owned economy are conducive to the entry of the property rights of state-owned assets into the market to achieve the circulation and reorganization of the property rights. In this way the ownership of state-owned assets can be integrated and unified, and the structure of state-owned assets can be optimized. This is the important point for the combination of the state-owned economy and the market economy.

Under the premise of not changing the state's ownership, the reform of the state-owned property rights system is, in the final analysis, a question of how to establish procedures for entrusting, and the trustee system. The "entrusting-trustee" is a difficult question that has long puzzled both Chinese and foreign theore-

CHAPTER III REFORM OF THE PROPERTY RIGHTS SYSTEM

ticians. It is even more so for state-owned property rights. As the state, which cannot directly exercise the owner's power and function, must choose an agent or agents to exercise it, one of the difficult questions is: Who is the ultimate entruster, namely, who has the power to decide who can and cannot exercise state-owned property rights? Of course, in reality it is usually the concerned state organ which exercises the owner's power and function on behalf of the state. In this case, the "entruster" has, in fact, become an agent. The second question arising from this is: Who restrains the "entruster" in form in the absence of an ultimate entruster? Especially when the "entruster" is directly related to the rights and interests of the owner, the entruster of the "ownerless" assets will be hard to decide. The third difficult question is: Even if the status of the entruster is established through legal procedure, the interests of the entruster and of the trustee contradict each other. The former often departs from the principle of maximum profit in order to pursue political interests and interfere with the trustee, while the latter is hindered from pursuing economic achievements by a lack of adequate power. Behind the above three questions lies the fourth difficult question: In the multi-leveled "entrusting-trustee" relationship, in the absence of an ultimate entruster, either the "entruster" or the "trustee" has no material foundation for assuming responsibility for the failure of management, thus reducing their interest in the "entrusting-trustee" assets.

Experience in the reform of state-owned property rights in recent years has shown that many forms can be adopted to separate state-owned property rights (or public property rights) from ownership, but the property rights main body should be most desirably the enterprises. Enterprises are mainly entrusted to manage state-owned assets (or collective assets), and by gradually establishing a modern enterprise system to ensure that enterprises can effectively exercise their property rights.

A correct concept of cost should be formed in the course of changing the state-owned property rights system. The state pays to maintain the existing system and likewise pays the cost of creating a new system. The fundamental difference between them is that the former only prolongs the life of the existing system while the latter will become an efficient new system. Therefore, in this process, part of state-owned assets are used to clear the debts of the old system once and for all and cultivate the growth of the new system. This is the price we must pay to create the new property rights system. In this way, not only will there be no question of losing state-owned assets, but, on the contrary, it will be the indispensable means for stopping further losses of state-owned assets.

(II) Complete property rights refer to the legal, full, and actual rights of the main body to control the assets it manages.

Commodity exchange includes the competitive selling and buying activities between the parties to the exchange. Such exchange activities and the formation of competitive market prices as their result are presupposed by the possession of the products or currency by the parties to the exchange. The concept of property rights here is in the broadest sense, namely, the main body's exclusive right to control an object. It includes ownership and the actual right to control it. It is not difficult to understand that the activities of market exchange are presupposed by the main body's property rights. Because so far as the seller is concerned, if he can sell the product he brings to the market effectively through competition, he must be the true controller of the product. If what he has is the property of another person or a stolen article, he has no right to sell it, and if he sells it, it is an unlawful act and an invalid transaction. As to the buyer, if he wants to carry out an effective purchase through competition he must have money in his pocket or another product for the exchange, and the money or product must be owned or controlled by him independently. In other words, he must also be a holder of the property rights. It can thus be seen that the main body's property rights are the prerequisite and foundation for market activities. Since the property rights set the conditions for exchange activities, we can conclude that the nature of these rights decides the nature of the exchange. In concrete, if there are

CHAPTER III REFORM OF THE PROPERTY RIGHTS SYSTEM

incomplete and unclear property rights, there follows an incomplete exchange of commodities; but if there are maturely developed and clearly defined property rights, there will follow a still more developed exchange of commodities.

As to the formation of prices, market mechanisms will tend to strike a balance between price and value. With this, the participants will adapt to the market and tend to compete as equals. The main body's production and business activities are impossible without a system structure, and particularly the structure of the property rights system. It can be said that a complete property rights structure is the foundation for market activities.

Complete property rights refer to the main body's legal, full and actual rights to independently control and manage assets under its operation. Concretely these rights include: a. actual controlling rights; b. incompatible controlling right; c. full controlling rights; and d. legal controlling rights.

(1) Actual controlling rights.

Actual controlling rights refer to the fact that the main body has the real and independent right to control a thing or an object. People can have or use a thing, but cannot control it independently, so they cannot use it for exchange. Therefore, the commodity nature and marketization of the economy call for the granting of actual controlling rights to all sorts of main bodies. For example, workers will have the actual right to control their labor and scientists, technicians, writers, and artists will have the actual right to control their intellectual products. This is the prerequisite for the emergence of exchange of production elements and for the formation and development of all market elements.

(2) Incompatible controlling right.

The incompatibility and unsuper impossibility of the rights are the characteristics of the complete property rights. If one thing has several or many owners and every one of them has the right to control it, in fact no one can have the right to control the thing as the owner of the property. In that case, people cannot use the thing effectively in production. It is because of this, to establish property rights without incompatible main bodies is the prerequisite for the market development.

(3) Full controlling rights.

Complete property rights are generally demonstrated by the possession of complete ownership: The right to control the object, the right to the profits from the property, and the right to handle the property are the three-dimension structure of these powers and functions. The concrete forms of these three-dimensional property rights vary. Complete property rights draw support from the effective right to control, the full right to profit, and the necessary right to handle property to ensure the main body's full rights, interest, and responsibility in the use and management of assets.

(4) Legal property rights.

Complete property rights are safeguarded by law and are therefore secured. Legal guarantees and restrictions are the prerequisite for safeguarding and ensuring property ownership in an economic world filled with conflicts of interest. They also safeguard the very complicated rights of diverse groups with regard to the rights of ownership, profit, and disposal of property, and creditor's rights in a modern market economy with ever more complicated relations and interests. These are the legal conditions for the micro main body organization of independent production. Legal property rights, through the standardization of market behavior, form production and market order as well as the fair competition mechanism. The latter is an essential lever for realizing market mechanisms. So we can conclude that legal property rights play an essential role in promoting and strengthening those mechanisms.

In short, the main body's economic behavior is subject to the structure of property rights.

III. The Issue of the Central and Local Publicly Owned Assets

(I) Separate property rights systems for the central and local governments should be established as part of a coordinated effort to solve the conflict of interest between the central

CHAPTER III REFORM OF THE PROPERTY RIGHTS SYSTEM

and local governments.

Some experts support the idea of separating the property rights of state-owned assets into two systems: Those of the central government and those of the local governments. Their reasons are as follows:

Because of China's vast size and diversity, the development level of productivity can vary greatly from place to place. The situations in the provinces and counties are complex, and if this reality is not given full consideration in regulating ownership and management it will be difficult to guarantee the effective operation of these assets. Moreover, it would be counterproductive to the mobilization of local initiative and creativity.

In light of the actual conditions in China, state-owned assets are, in fact, already divided into "centrally managed assets" and "locally managed assets," and income from state-owned assets is further separated into "central income" and "local income." Establishment of a local system of public ownership is simply a recognition of already existing reality.

Formal recognition of this situation would bring great benefits to the practical operations of these enterprises. First and foremost, it would benefit mutual competition of state-owned assets under a socialist market economy. This is an important factor in giving impetus to the rational allocation and optimization of state-owned assets. Second, it would be conducive to instilling a real sense of responsibility for state-owned assets in all aspects. Third, it will benefit the rational flow of property rights in the market.

Two methods may be adopted to establish publicly owned property rights for the localities. The first is to separate ownership between the central and local governments. Central investment would belong to the central government, local investment would belong to the local governments, and mixed investments would be divided according to the respective proportion of investment. The other method would be for the central government to entrust the local governments with the control of assets owned by the central government.

Some experts contend that the separation of ownership between the central and local governments is, in essence, simply a classification of proxy relationships.

When discussing relationships within ownership by the whole people, we face a question: Does property belonging to the whole people actually belong to the whole people, or to the state? It makes no difference whether it is the central government or the local governments; because both act as agents for people's property. What we are in fact discussing then are financial relationships, of the central government acting on behalf of the whole people as administrator of property accumulated through several decades of labor by the entire workforce. Adoption of a separation of proxy management will make it easier to form a competitive market for capital accumulation. The value of property owned by the whole people is presently distorted under the planned economic system, and many essential production capabilities have been developed regardless of price and were, in fact, created by the labor of the entire nation. Some entrepreneurs argue that their enterprises have never received state investment, that their capital accumulation that has been due to loans should belong to the employees of those enterprises. But in fact, under the planned economy and because of price distortions, enterprise assets embody a scissors movement of prices obtained from the peasants, and price differences arising from resource-oriented enterprises, including an increase in land value resulting from China's large-scale infrastructure construction. This value cannot be said to have been created by an enterprise's workers—all of the assets owned by the whole people has been created by the concerted efforts of civilians over the past decades. However, due to the high degree of centralization of our agent system, a competitive market economy has been unable to take shape. Therefore, a system of separate agent powers should be adopted for property owned by the whole people; namely, a portion managed directly by the central government with local governments exercising administrative power over another portion, and so on down to administration by the local communities. With these groups acting as the original investors, new financial relationships may be

CHAPTER III REFORM OF THE PROPERTY RIGHTS SYSTEM

installed among enterprises. Moreover, a corporate system, including a board of directors exercising true control over assets, may be established. Only by rationalizing and streamlining relations at these two levels can China form a truly competitive system of capital operation.

(II) To differentiate between the property rights of the central government and those of local governments is to redefine property relations that are not in conformity with the principles of efficiency.

One issue facing the present process of reform of property rights relationships is whether or not to redifferentiate between property rights of the central government and those of the local governments.

On this question, the argument often made by those who say that localities and enterprises should be given a share of the property rights is: "Give to the state what the state has invested, give to the localities what the localities have invested, and give to enterprises what the enterprises have themselves amassed." This formula is simply unworkable. First, in principle, as long as the manager and staff have received a reasonable salary, benefits, and other compensation, and the enterprise has paid its debts, the remainder accumulation of assets should find its way back to the original investors or owners, i.e., the state. Second, in the fixed arrangement of property rights in the past, local governments were subordinate to the central government. This was termed "level-classified management" of state-owned assets with "professional supervision" over the operational activities of state-owned enterprises. This, in principle, was equivalent to modified management with no power of expropriation over the remainder of accumulated assets. They were not the primary ownership organizations and therefore were unable to share in property rights.

However, the question that now concerns us is not past property rights arrangements but rather how to reform these relationships to make them more effective. In the fixed arrangement of property rights in the past some things may not make sense; but, as to the goals and demands of market reform and to more effective property rights arrangements, these same things are quite rational. Simultaneously, since under the past system most rights, responsibilities and benefits were not defined beforehand—a vast "fuzzy area"—and were eventually termed "surplus rights" (such as "non-contractual rights") belonging to the central government, many problems arose with regards to efficiency. This is in need of transformation, and we now need to redefine the past relations of property rights which do not accord with the principle of efficiency.

1. Experience has demonstrated that public assets in the hands of the nation as a whole, acting as owner, is a system that has failed. This was the former system of property rights, and now we must search for a new arrangement, no matter who the assets belonged to in the past.

2. Under this past ownership arrangement many relationships were unclear. Income that should have gone to the central government was in fact often grabbed by the localities, which the central government was unable to control. Often a locality would enjoy the income from these assets, but would not take responsibility for losses. In the end, losses were absorbed by the central government and chalked up on the state's tab. It thus would be best if these rights were given to the localities; they would then not only enjoy the benefits but would also bear the responsibility for any losses, lightening the burden on the central government. From the central government's perspective, it is not necessary to control assets in order to control the economy. It may be more effective to use methods such as taxes and macroeconomic adjustment policies. Therefore, giving property rights to the localities can be used in place of local taxes and the localities can secure some rights over assets while increasing the proportion of taxes collected by the central government.

3. Experience has also shown that a small-scale publicly owned economy is more effective than a large-scale one because it can at least consolidate the distances between the ultimate owner, the agent of the property rights, and the de facto operating

CHAPTER III REFORM OF THE PROPERTY RIGHTS SYSTEM

agent.

4. By giving a portion of enterprise property rights to the locality and making enterprises only partially state-owned budget restrictions are strengthened and dependency on state banks is lessened. In general, township enterprises have good economic returns. Because it is more difficult for them to obtain loans from the bank than it is for state-owned enterprises. So township enterprises must depend on themselves.

5. By the time the localities acquire property rights these rights will already have been diversified. This will result from the demands of a market economy, aiding competition and development. It will also facilitate the trading of property rights, bringing about the redistribution of assets among various and diverse operations and operating systems.

6. When the localities are given property rights and large numbers of enterprises are no longer state owned, the state will be able to allow others to run management for the profit of everyone.

7. At present, there are two methods by which property rights may appropriately be given to localities. One is for local enterprises to be placed under local administration. The other is to place a portion of the property rights to state-owned enterprises under local administration. This method would encourage the transformation of the enterprise system itself, though transformation is presently encountering strong resistance because, from the enterprises' perspective, they have nothing to gain. The localities also feel that transformation will bring no advantage to them. The central government has already yielded a certain amount of authority during this reform process. If it can go a step further and give up some property rights, this will certainly promote changes within the current property rights system.

8. When the localities gain property rights this will bring about special benefits. It will place the risks of reform within the localities, relieving the central government of the burden. This entire process will enhance the gradual transformation of public assets, and from a long-term perspective, will help dispel risks, bring about greater social stability, give the localities property

rights, and reduce social problems that naturally appear in the course of reform.

IV. Establishing the Property Rights of the Labor Force Under the Socialist Market Economy

(I) The question of the property rights of the labor force.

Reform of the property rights system within China's state-owned enterprises directly touches on problems of three magnitudes. First, the establishment of a system of public ownership has the advantage of standardizing the behavior of the holders of public assets while simultaneously establishing a strong foundation for the rational circulation of property rights. Second, the founding of corporate ownership helps enterprises assume responsibility for their assets and become truly independent entities in the market place. Third, the establishment of property rights of the labor force would help correct relations between workers and enterprises. Through a system of rewards these workers could attain the dual status of both worker and owner Marx related. Reform of the property rights system must resolve the problems in these three areas. The goal is to rationally standardize relations between the government, enterprises, and workers, allowing each to pursue its own interests while simultaneously shouldering its responsibilities.

The "property rights of the labor force" refers not only to the salary earned by the worker but also to a certain degree of income earned through property rights. For example, a portion of an enterprise's profits may be converted into stock then given to the workers on the basis of their production value, time, responsibilities, contributions, and other factors. Stock obtained through these property rights would be non-transferable, non-exchangeable, and non-inheritable. In practice, to acknowledge the property rights of the labor force is to fully implement the labor theory of value. In the overall development of a socialist market economy, the property rights of the labor force is of the

CHAPTER III REFORM OF THE PROPERTY RIGHTS SYSTEM

utmost importance.

(II) Establishment of labor's property rights must be accomplished through coordination of the interests of both enterprises and laborers forming a long-term, stable mechanism for development of state-owned enterprises.

Basically, enterprise reform is to adjust rational interests between enterprises and workers, allowing both sides to realize the maximum benefits possible. With continuing reform, the traditional balance of interests is no longer suitable for transition toward a market economy as contradictions in enterprises become more and more apparent. During this process of economic transition conflicts between the interests of enterprises and workers are becoming more prominent with each passing day.

(1) The conflicts between the interests of workers, enterprises, and the state. Under the traditional planned economy the state utilized a highly centralized form of management over workers' salaries. The interests of the enterprise's staff and workers were represented by the state, with the workers relying on enterprises and the enterprises relying on the state. Meanwhile, the allocation of factors of production (including the labor force) mainly relied on administrative means. Distribution was handled according to an extreme egalitarianism which covered up the conflict between a multiplicity of interests. Under this system it was impossible to form methods for handling the property rights interests among the state, enterprises, and workers.

The quest for the most effective use of state-owned assets and maximum profit, and the quest of the workers for maximum personal benefits are both necessary components of the market economy. With the smashing of the "iron rice bowl" the marketization of laborers, laborers will seek those jobs that most benefit them personally. At present, because of a variety of restrictions, there is a great degree of fluidity within the labor force. At the same time, their skill level is increasing, the mobility of trained personnel is growing and some highly skilled technical personnel is now moving into general management positions and labor-intensive enterprises. The high mobility of the present labor force can have positive effects in optimizing the distribution of human resources. At the same time we must take into consideration the negative impact this movement among the workers could have on the interests of enterprise and the state. Resolving the problem of property rights for labor will entail a long-term unification of the interests of labor, enterprises, and the state—a gradual formation of a common body inclusive of state, collective, and individual interests.

Transferring a portion of enterprise profits to the income of workers will help unify the interests of both parties and forcefully promote increased economic efficiency. Therefore, the essence of labor's property rights is not simply to put state-owned assets in the hands of individuals, much less is it a system of privatization. In fact, by implementing these rights the conflict between the two interests can be correctly handled, aiding the expansion and stabilization of income from state-owned assets and providing long-term, effective guarantees to the state as owner.

(2) The conflict between short-term and long-term interests. Economic experience has revealed a direct relationship between the short-term actions of enterprises and the excessive desire for personal short-term gain on the part of workers, particularly operating managers, to the extent that enterprises often offer short-term wage incentives to their workers. In the early stages of the transition from a planned to a market economy, it is impossible to avoid the workers' desire to maximize personal gain, but excessive eagerness for immediate gain may harm the long-term interests of enterprises and workers alike.

A system in which employees become stockholders would closely tie workers' income with the enterprise's profits and losses, thereby changing the formerly rigid wage system. As a result, staff and workers will take great interest in the welfare of the enterprise, strengthening their participation in management and policy formation. Both workers and enterprises would then share the same fate. In this way perhaps a workable solution can be found to the conflict between long-term and short-term interests.

CHAPTER III REFORM OF THE PROPERTY RIGHTS SYSTEM

(3) The conflict between the input of currency capital and that of labor capital in the distribution of interests. For some time now we have unilaterally taken the input of currency capital as increases in economic benefits, while skipping over the important function of labor capital. There is a large difference in the returns of currency capital input and labor capital input, but this disparity easily results in the laborers using every opportunity and method to seek short-term gains from currency capital input. Especially in the initial transition to a market economy, this phenomenon has a certain universality.

Capital property rights are concerned with large returns through the input of material resources capital, while labor force property rights are mainly concerned with the input of labor capital. To achieve the organization and creation of factors of all kinds of resources through the organic blending of material capital and manpower capital will raise worker productiveness and secure corresponding returns. With the continual development of modern socialist production, the effects of manpower capital are growing more pronounced.

The present lack of quality and responsibility in management has already impaired enterprise effectiveness. Especially since the establishment of the enterprise property rights system, the role of managers has become more important than ever. The problems inherent in the current management of Chinese state-owned enterprises are manifold. Many of these problems have a direct relationship with the substandard ability of the managers themselves. To make these managers more effective it is necessary for China to reform the operational management systems and to resolve the problem of the irrational distribution of the interests of managers. In maximizing the use of human resources, it is important to emphasize and develop the special role of enterprise managers. In resolving the problem of labor force property rights it is necessary to handle better the labor force rights among managers. This is very important for the reform and development of enterprises.

(III) The need to resolve the property rights of the labor force

is a universal problem in the market economy.

With the development and socialization of production, human resources are becoming more and more important. Over the last 20 years many Western countries with market economies have adopted expansive partnership systems and employee-held stock plans devoted to coordinating relations between labor and capital and promoting economic growth.

The employee-held stock plan was first proposed in the 1960s by a famous American lawyer. The basic idea is to give employees a financial stake in the company. After this method was introduced it was quickly adopted by many Western countries. Currently, the United States has more than 1,000 publicly owned companies with employee-held stock plans. England, while in the process of de-socialization, saw over 90 percent of those companies adopting the employee-held stock system. In Japan, of the 2,719 listed companies, 1,943 of them had used this system by 1990. The employee-held stock plan can be locked upon as a system wherein the labor supplied by the workers empowers them to share in the company's stock. This destroys at the base the centralized monopoly of capital and furthers the development of labor's share in capital. It provides workers with a channel for sharing profits by their work, skills, and knowledge, and is therefore a step up from allowing workers to simply purchase stock.

China is currently transforming from a traditional planned economy to a socialist market economy. How it effectively solves the problem of labor force property rights will determine the balance of economic relations within enterprises. While promoting the reform of state-owned enterprises, China must learn from effective examples in those countries with market economies while giving expression to the socialist nature of the market economy within China.

First, labor force property rights should be as broad as possible and, whether in the state or non-state sector, these rights should encompass all workers.

Second, labor force property rights must realize a compati-

CHAPTER III REFORM OF THE PROPERTY RIGHTS SYSTEM

bility of interests. The establishment of these rights must take into consideration the interests of the state, collectives, and individuals. Moreover, it must comprehensively link long-term and short-term interests. Only in this way will the establishment of labor force property rights assist continued economic growth, guarantee the status of the socialist public sector, guarantee the status of vast numbers of workers as the masters of enterprises, and secure the development of state-owned enterprises on a long-term and reliable foundation.

Third, labor force property rights must have a rational dissimilarity. Establishment of labor force property rights is a revolution in distribution under the socialist market economy. It offers an effective mechanism for the encouragement of an optimum combination of material and human resources, brings about maximum efficiency, and provides a motivational foundation for the long-term development of enterprises. Simultaneously, the fact that the rewards obtained by a worker under labor force property rights are tied to work performance will encourage large numbers of workers to improve their productivity, thereby strengthening competitiveness and more fully developing the capability of human resources.

Fourth, labor force rights must be established while maintaining the unity of efficiency and fairness. The establishment of labor force rights must truly follow the principle of equally considering efficiency and fairness. The uneven quality of the labor force exists objectively and these differences should be reflected in the incomes gained through labor force property rights. It is imperative to avoid a return to the egalitarian "iron rice bowl" of the past.

(IV) While speeding up the reform of state-owned enterprises, China should keep searching for new ways to realize labor force property rights, and gradually spread experiences to the greater whole.

In the past two years, with the deepening of enterprise reform, a minority of enterprises have already begun experimenting with the stock system and are searching for other ways to extend property rights to the labor force. Although these limited measures are still in their infancy, they have nonetheless provided practical experience in the resolution of this problem. State-owned enterprises are now accelerating the transition to a corporate system, which presents the best opportunity for realizing labor force property rights. During the transition to a corporate system we must emphasize research and adopt flexible solutions for a variety of situations among enterprises.

—In the transition to a stock system, large state-owned enterprises may determine the proportion of profits allocated to the labor force through comprehensive consultations.

—Some small state-owned enterprises may implement a system of state-owned public operation, thereby allowing the labor force to secure a somewhat larger portion. Those state-owned enterprises with serious losses will be able to increase the labor force's proportion by gradually unifying the interests of all parties and resolving the problem of losses.

—Some enterprises that were originally collectives can use labor force property rights to create broader worker interests, changing the enterprise into the worker's own.

At present, one feasibility method would be to select a few enterprises which are currently implementing the stock system as pilot projects to monitor labor force property rights reform. In the past, this problem was addressed by attempts to install a system of stock for employees. Although the stock system served an important function in raising funds, it was unable to effectively solve the problem, and workers and enterprises failed to develop a merging of interests. In the majority of these enterprises, due to the changes in the system of stocks for employees, it therefore was difficult to form a common interests. Also, workers eagerly used a variety of methods to transfer their own stocks, even though regulations stipulated that transfers could not be made for several years. Not only were these regulations unreasonable, they could not be readily enforced. In any case, after several years these stocks were to become public stock. Therefore, the property rights of labor and employees holding internal stocks

CHAPTER III REFORM OF THE PROPERTY RIGHTS SYSTEM

were not exactly the same thing. An enterprise issues stock, which acts as a financial commodity that anyone has the right to purchase on the open market. Moreover, these stocks can be transferred according to regulations. An enterprise's stock is then accorded a variety of artificial identities, such as "employee-held internal stocks," or "social public stocks," etc. This, in fact, creates all kinds of problems.

Pilot projects carrying out property rights reform may adopt a variety of methods such as collective trust holding companies, individual account holding companies, employee holding associations and the like. Considering the current situation, the initial adoption of trust funds or employee holding associations would probably be the safest ways to begin.

It also means that the property right to the labor power of the staff and workers shall be owned collectively by the trust funds, and the annual profit from this labor shall be decided according to work produced or by the combination of the collective trust funds and individual holding, and then shifted to personal accounts when conditions are ripe. In the pilot projects, attention should be paid to the following questions: Egalitarian distribution, which makes it difficult to arouse employees' enthusiasm; and short-term behavior, i.e., the quantification of the labor property right to all employees without leaving any margin, would make it even more difficult to change labor property rights. The percentage of these rights in the distribution of enterprise profit is relatively stable, but income earned by employees varies because of different jobs, contributions and work time.

The combination of enterprises and employees, preconditioned by the relations of interests, is an important goal pursued universally under modern market economic conditions. Since we practice a socialist market economy we should handle relations between these two interests even better to give lasting motive force to the socialist market economy and achieve the goal of common prosperity. Therefore, the introduction of labor property rights is an important part of the reform of state-owned enterprises and is of important practical significance for establishing the socialist market economy system.

V. Property Rights Market: Advancing the Circulation and Reorganization of Property Rights

(I) The necessity of transferring and reorganizing the property rights of state-owned assets.

The resources of economic operations are mainly concentrated within the enterprises, manifesting themselves as various production elements. If the market is to be the foundation for allocating resources, all production elements must be put into the market and regulated through the market. Capital is an important production element and it too must be circulated in the market in order to achieve optimum allocation. One important form the circulation and reorganization of capital takes is the circulation and reorganization of property rights. Through this circulation and reorganization we can push forward and achieve capital reorganization.

The circulation and reorganization of the property rights of state-owned enterprises is an important way to reasonably allocate state-owned resources and optimize the state-owned capital structure. Optimization of the state-owned capital structure can lead to the adjustment of distribution and the industrial structure. Product mix and new organizational structure will improve efficiency and strengthen the entire state-owned economy.

By promoting changes in the property rights structure in an orderly way and wisely choosing the organizational form of enterprise properties while utilizing the role of state-owned capital, we can make better use of the leading role of the state-owned economy and expand its influence.

We will also be able to make coherent inventories of accumulated state-owned assets and use this to solve the current contradictions of over-employment and under-use of state-owned enterprises. We must explore avenues for solving the problem of debt and social burdens within state-owned enterprises through the

CHAPTER III REFORM OF THE PROPERTY RIGHTS SYSTEM

reorganization of assets and liabilities, speed up the process of establishing a modern enterprise system, and increase the vigor of these enterprises.

The circulation and reorganization of property rights within the state-owned economy can adjust the relations of property and interest among the central government, local governments and governmental departments. This is conducive to a reasonable distribution of state-owned assets and to the coordination of relations between the central government and local governments.

In the course of establishing the socialist market economy, the transfer and reorganization of state-owned assets property rights is extremely important for the development of the capital market and the property rights market. The investment organs or the departments authorized by the state are the principals in transactions of state-owned property rights. The enterprises as investors are also holders of the property rights of the enterprises in which they invest. These property rights holders are also the principals of the property rights markets. Only with their active participation can the property rights markets be developed.

(II) The principles that should be observed and the foundation work that must be done in the circulation and reorganization of the property rights of state-owned assets.

There are two ways in which the property rights of state-owned assets are circulated by readjustment and by transfer. Readjustment is the act of altering the relations of authorization by the state according to law and changing the investors of state-owned assets, thus adjusting the relations of subordination of the power and interests of state-owned capital. This can only be done within the state-owned economy. Transfer is the act of transferring the power and interests of state-owned capital by the investors of state-owned assets with compensation. This can be done either within or outside the state-owned economy. Both methods should be employed in the course of establishing the socialist market economy.

The circulation and reorganization of the property rights of state-owned assets must adhere to the following principles: Earnestly safeguarding the state's power and interests and ensuring the preserved and increased value of state-owned assets; optimizing the structure of state-owned assets; giving play to the leading role of the state-owned economy; making full use of market mechanisms; making comprehensive inventories of state-owned assets; and observing the laws in a standard way.

In the course of transferring the property rights of state-owned assets, it is essential to adhere to the principles that the transfer shall be made with compensation according to law, that assets be evaluated, that prices be decided by the market, and that income from the transfer shall be used for reinvestment as state-owned capital.

When transferring the property rights of state-owned assets it is essential to take inventory of the assets in enterprises with state-owned capital, verify the amount of property possessed by the enterprise, define property rights, decide the investors of state-owned capital, evaluate the assets, divide the floating from the non-floating assets, clarify debts receivable and debts payable, and handle the debt burdens left over from the past in order to shift the examination of assets to a financial and accounting system suitable to the needs of a market economy. Moreover, it is necessary to establish a system of responsibility for the management of state-owned assets and define the rights, obligations and responsibilities of the investors and users of state-owned capital. It is also necessary to perfect legislation for the circulation and reorganization of the property rights of state-owned assets, set up market medium organizations for asset evaluation and auditing, cultivate the property rights markets and establish a system for supervising state-owned assets.

(III) Many problems remain in our theoretical knowledge of and experience in market operations for the circulation and reorganization of the property rights of enterprises, particularly state-owned enterprises.

1. Who is main body of responsible for the circulation and reorganization of the property rights of enterprises? State-owned

CHAPTER III REFORM OF THE PROPERTY RIGHTS SYSTEM

assets in China are represented by the central government and supervised at different levels. This is clear insofar as ownership of state-owned assets is concerned. However, for the circulation and reorganization of enterprises' property rights, it is necessary to establish an independent property right for the enterprise corporation. This is the independent market operator of the enterprise corporation as a whole. Therefore, its market principal should be the enterprise corporation, namely, the organ or organization which can act or decide on it behalf to dispose of the property of the enterprise, and has the power to decide the circulation and reorganization of the enterprise property rights. In concrete words, it is the meeting of shareholders, the board of directors, or the enterprise's corresponding organ of power. If power and responsibility are not clearly defined in this way and everything must be approved and decided by the representative of the ultimate owner, it will be impossible to maintain an efficient market operation.

2. Marketization of asset evaluation. Reasonable and lawful asset evaluation is the foundation for the circulation and reorganization of the property rights of state-owned enterprises. For the state-owned enterprises, it is necessary to reserve the right of final confirmation of the management department of state-owned assets. The guiding principle and method of evaluation should be based on marketization. For example, when the assets of an old state-owned enterprise are evaluated, its machinery, equipment and other assets no longer have much value under market conditions because of antiquated plants and other factors (though they still have some value based on the percentage of modernity) while its intangible assets, such as the factory name, brand name, trademark and management network still have large market potential. So there is a question of asset evaluation. We must take the evaluation of state-owned assets into account in order to reflect its real value.

3. Marketized operation of the circulation and reorganization of the property rights. The price of property rights fixed by the evaluation of assets is, in fact, a reference price in the operation of the market. In actual operation, at auction for example, a

transaction may be made at a price perhaps higher or lower than the evaluated price. This conforms to the law of the market economy. In fact, there arises a question of how to correctly evaluate which state-owned assets are lost. We should end the artificial loss of state-owned assets. But when business organs handling state-owned assets or state-owned enterprises, in order to suit the need of the market competition, adopt the market operational method of adjusting or taking inventory of existing state-owned assets, this should not be regarded as a loss of state-owned assets. We must see and evaluate the circulation and reorganization of each specific property right in light of development. The objective laws to be observed are the laws of the market economy, and the core question is to truly fix responsibility for state-owned assets.

When an enterprise joins the market independently and becomes an operative in the market, the method of circulating and reorganizing property rights becomes an important strategic policy decision facing enterprise managers. When the enterprise needs to rapidly expand production, raise its market share, and reduce the number of rivals, the most effective shortcut is to purchase other enterprises in order to strengthen itself. When the enterprise wants to make an important adjustment to its product mix but is seriously short of assets, it can auction or transfer part of its property rights to gain capital funds for investment in the most needed projects.

The circulation and reorganization of an enterprise's property rights breaks away from the limits of industries, trades, regions and forms of ownership. In this way everything can be put to the service of the fundamental goal of all enterprises—creating ever higher economic results.

Chapter IV
The Transformation of State-Owned Enterprises Under a Corporate System

I. Reform of State-Owned Enterprises of Various Types and a Model for Corporate System Transformation

(I) **State-owned enterprises should be transformed in four categories in light of their circumstances:**

The first category. Those state-owned enterprises which have long suffered losses, whose assets cannot offset their liabilities, and whose technology is obsolete and products unmarketable should declare bankruptcy.

Because state-owned enterprises from their inception have been able to survive by eating from the "big cauldron" of the state regardless of product marketability or profit and lose, none of them could be closed for any reason. As a result, the efficiency of many enterprises has constantly declined with large quantities of products overstocked and an amazing loss of funds and resources. Not only do these enterprises themselves have serious difficulties, but they directly or indirectly affect the operation of the entire economy. Declaring bankruptcy and closing these enterprises will not only reduce the useless waste and alleviate the shortage of social funds, but it will also improve the efficiency of state-owned enterprises as a whole, lighten the pressure of inflation, and even diminish difficulties for the whole economy. Facts show that if an enterprise goes bankrupt even unemployment security and relief provided to the staff and workers becomes much less than the price the state now must pay to continue this present fruitless production.

The second category. The large number of small state-owned enterprises can be turned gradually into enterprises not owned by the state through transformation, stock, leasing, and sales.

China now has 200,000-300,000 state-owned industrial and commercial enterprises, of which only about 10,000 are large and medium-sized. There are many more small enterprises which are necessary to social and economic development. But their assets are not large nor do they employ great numbers of workers. Whether in the structure of ownership or in economic life in general they do not play decisive role. Moreover, most of them are poorly managed and the burdens imposed on them are very heavy with a large proportion suffering losses. The income of their employees and the degree of social security are also low. A better and more feasible solution is for the state to gradually exit from these fields and turn them into enterprises not owned or operated by the state. For example, some of them can be turned into enterprises owned collectively by employees, some can be turned into stock-holding enterprises by pooling employee stock, some may be sold at auction to become non-public enterprises, and some leased or owned by the state but operated privately. This will not only effectively increase the vigor of these enterprises, improve their results, increase state revenues and reduce state subsidies, but will also greatly save wasted government energy at all levels and enable the leadership to concentrate on developing and reforming the large and medium-sized state-owned enterprises.

Preliminary practical experience in some areas has shown that reform aimed at gradually turning small state-owned enterprises into non-state enterprises has narrowed the scope of state ownership. This is in fact a reasonable adjustment of the enterprise structure. Not only is it greatly conducive to the development of enterprises and productive forces, but it also benefits the state, society, and workers alike.

The third category. Ordinary medium-sized enterprises can be turned into enterprises with mixed ownership through joint ventures or cooperative enterprises.

There are a great number of enterprises in this category

CHAPTER IV TRANSFORMATION UNDER A CORPORATE SYSTEM

among large and medium-sized enterprises in China. They also need much revision and face many difficulties in the course of reform. Therefore, through the circulation and reorganization of property rights we can firstly change these enterprises into ones with mixed ownership. This can be accomplished by taking inventory of assets, pooling funds from village-run enterprises, collective enterprises, overseas investors, public organizations, corporations, and private enterprises. The enterprises shall then no longer have responsibility for taking care of all the needs of their employees.

The fourth category. The large and medium-sized key state-owned enterprises shall be transformed under the corporate system more quickly and in a standard way, and a modern enterprise system shall be gradually set up for the development of modern production and the market economy.

This is the focal point for the reform of state-owned enterprises, as well as the crucial question of whether economic reform in China can surmount all barriers and achieve ultimate success. The general principle for reform is: Adhering to public ownership while changing the traditional pattern of the state-owned economy. This is because China is a socialist country and the state will continue to hold in its hands and control those industries and enterprises which are vital to the national economy, no matter how the economic system changes. This is not only needed to maintain the leading role of the state-owned economy but also to keep the growth of the economy stable. Of course, whether state-owned enterprises can continue to play this role still depends, in the end, on high economic results and efficiency.

Both positive and negative experiences in the practice of economic development and reform in China during the past decades have shown that if state-owned enterprises are to play an effective role, we must make up our minds to realize systematic innovations in the structure of existing large and medium-sized key enterprises, apart from transforming medium-sized and small enterprises and abolishing fruitless enterprises. The major trend of reform is that under the provisions of the Company Law promulgated not long ago, the existing large and medium-sized key enterprises shall be gradually transformed into modern corporate enterprises with clearly defined property rights as the basis and a corporate system as the core. The modern corporate enterprise is characterized by the investors assuming limited liabilities and specialists assuming responsibility for management, and guaranteed by a scientific and reasonable administrative structure and management system. A few natural monopoly and special enterprises shall be reorganized into exclusive state-owned companies, most of them reorganized into limited liability companies, and some, if conditions permit, also reorganized into limited liability stock companies. The state can hold the controlling stock in some of the enterprises in the latter two categories, but will not hold controlling stock in others, depending on specific conditions. However, the total amount of state-owned and collective stock shall take the leading place as a whole. In the course of the reorganization, the establishment of the limited liability companies will be quicker, with the aim of changing the irrational old setup as quickly as possible. Limited liability stock companies will be established in a prudent way in order to avoid the loss of state-owned assets and chaos in the financial market resulting from defective work. Moreover, they must act according to international practices to ensure the property rights of these enterprises and healthy stock market growth. Although there are only several thousand of large and medium-sized key enterprises, they exert a major influence on the Chinese economy. As long as we make up our minds to reform these enterprises, we can anticipate not only that economic reform in China will make large strides forward, but that it also will forcefully promote the further rapid and healthy growth of the Chinese economy.

(II) **The way out for state-owned enterprises: A minority of them shall be reorganized in light of the modern enterprise system, and the majority shall be owned and operated nongovernmentally. Three categories of state-owned enterprises shall remain: The large and extra-large enterprises vital to the national economy, some new- and high-tech**

CHAPTER IV TRANSFORMATION UNDER A CORPORATE SYSTEM

industries, and public welfare services.

The state-owned enterprises in the above three categories can be reorganized into "limited liability companies" or "limited liability stock companies" patterned on the modern enterprise system within the limits of an unchanging and fundamental nature of state ownership. State-owned enterprises, after reorganization, shall be either companies with exclusive state capital or state holding companies which differ from their predecessors in three ways:

(1) The macro-environment has been changed from the previous planned economy to the new horizon of a market economy, thus making it possible to change the operating mechanisms;

(2) They were administrative units with unlimited liability in the past, and now there are limited liability companies, allowing the government to shake off the heavy burden of financial subsidies.

(3) They are freed from dependence on the government. With government administration separated from enterprise management, they find it possible to become truly independent enterprises making their own decisions.

The state-owned enterprises in the above three categories account for only a small percentage of the total. The majority of state-owned enterprises (mostly medium-sized and small enterprises) should be turned into privately owned or operated enterprises, gradually, through auction.

In the course developing the market economy there will certainly be many enterprises of "mixed blood," namely, economic mixtures of multiple ownership. Whether they are publicly owned, privately owned or mixtures of public and private ownership, the simultaneous vigorous development of the public and private sectors of the economy is an inevitable trend in the primary stage of socialism.

Whether the reform of state-owned enterprises can be carried out successfully also depends on whether we can correctly handle the following thorny questions:

1. The question of compensation for the employees of the

original state-owned enterprises.

The employees of the original state-owned enterprises have made contributions to their growth and compensation should be made to them all. This not only gives consideration to the interests of the employees, but also is conducive to the working class remaining the master of the enterprise.

2. The question of making arrangements for the placement of the unemployed.

After large numbers of state-owned enterprises are sold or reorganized, how shall we deal with large numbers of unemployed workers and staff members? This is of vital importance in determining whether the reform of state-owned enterprises can be carried out. The method of "buying up once and for all" can be used. For example, the management of the enterprise can pay 15,000 to 20,000 RMB yuan to each unemployed worker to end relations between the two parties. The unemployed can deposit the money with the social security departments which shall then take care of their social security affairs. Of course, this does not stop them from finding other jobs. The unemployed will also be exempt from participation in the social insurance system and can use the money any way they see fit.

3. The question of the liabilities of original state-owned enterprises.

Another difficult question arising from the reorganization of a minority of state-owned enterprises, and the shift from state ownership to private ownership and operation for a majority of state-owned enterprises is how to deal with the original liabilities of these enterprises. Since the responsible party of the old state-owned enterprises was the state, and the banks are also state-owned, the old liabilities should be settled by the state. Both the reorganized and auctioned state-owned enterprises should re-evaluate the enterprises' existing visible and invisible assets rather than get entangled in old debts. If there are endless disputes over liabilities reform cannot move forward.

(III) According to investigation and analysis, the reorganization of large enterprises under the corporate system in

CHAPTER IV TRANSFORMATION UNDER A CORPORATE SYSTEM

China now follows two patterns: The parallel decomposition pattern and the holding company pattern.

Large state-owned enterprises in China, products of the planned economy and "all-function" pattern, must carry on production and business operations, and must be engaged in auxiliary activities such as maintenance, building, and transport to solve the problems of supplementary services for their production and take care of the social needs of their employees. An all-inclusive "enterprise society" like this finds it impossible to enter the capital market and win acceptance by investors. Therefore, according to investigations made by specialists, when large enterprises are reorganized into stock companies they restructure their business, change their administrative pattern and transform production, business, and auxiliary systems into stock companies. All other production systems and non-production departments are separated from the stock companies and reorganized. At present, the patterns for the reorganization can be placed into two categories:

1. Parallel decomposition pattern.

The enterprises following this pattern have decomposed the original enterprises after reorganization into three mutually independent parts—stock companies, industrial corporations and other organs. The original enterprises then no longer exist. After their independence the first two parts both become independent legal persons and the third part is turned over to the communities or put temporarily under the care of the industrial corporations and turned over to the local governments when conditions are ripe. The Shanghai General Petrochemical Works (Jinshan General Petrochemical Works) followed this pattern when it was transformed into a stock company.

The Shanghai General Petrochemical Works was the largest petrochemical enterprise in China when it began in 1972. It was also the most profitable petrochemical enterprise. Since it is far from the city proper (75 kilometers from the city of Shanghai), the Jinshan area where the General Works is located is basically self-sufficient and forms a relatively comprehensive social community. The Shanghai General Petrochemical Works gained the attention of the world for its "speed" and "results." With approval of the relevant departments, the stock system was introduced into this extra-large enterprise in September 1992, and the General Petrochemical Works was broken up into three parts: One was organized into a limited stock company, embracing the refineries and chemical production plants and auxiliary production units, research units and business management departments, and issuing and marketing its stock within China and abroad. The second part was organized into the Jinshan Industrial Company, a service company providing services both to stockholding enterprises and to society as a whole. The original building enterprises, machinery maintenance systems, and motor transport systems were separated from the stock company and turned over to the industrial company. The third part included the departments and units which had exercised the administrative functions of government, such as the public security, the courts, the procuratorate, hospitals, schools, and shops employing a total of 11,000 staff and workers. They now practice independent business accounting and are temporarily under the auspices of the Jinshan Industrial Company. They will be turned over to the municipal government of Shanghai when conditions are ripe.

The limited stock company organized on the basis of the main production plants of the former petrochemical works has registered capital of 6.23 billion RMB yuan, including 62 percent in state-owned stock, 27 percent in foreign stock, 2.4 percent in domestic corporate stock and 2.4 percent in stock held by its former employees (including those turned over to other units). The stock issued to individuals other than former employees amount to 250 million yuan, accounting for 4 percent.

The representative of the state-owned stockholders is the China Petrochemical Corporation which exercises control over state-owned assets on behalf of the state, appoints its directors, and enjoys the rights of stockholder under the company's regulations. The relationship between the CPC and the stock company is no longer one between upper and lower levels, but one between stockholder and enterprise.

CHAPTER IV TRANSFORMATION UNDER A CORPORATE SYSTEM

The relationship between the China Petrochemical Corporation (CPC) and the General Industrial Company is the same as that between the CPC and the former Shanghai General Petrochemical Works. The CPC acts as the administrative department in charge of the General Industrial Company. The CPC makes up any losses suffered by the General Industrial Company and sets aside 200 million yuan a year from dividends turned over to the Ministry of Finance as a subsidy for the company's losses. In return, the CPC demands that the industrial company turn their losses into profits in three years. As to whether any subsidy will be given to an enterprise with losses after three years, that decision will be made in the future.

An agreement has been reached between the Stock Company and the Industrial Company on maintaining the traditional relationship between supply and demand. Under the same conditions, the stock company shall give priority to using the services provided by the industrial company and give all necessary support to the industrial company. Any other measures must be approved unanimously at the meeting of investors, and the stock company is prohibited from shifting its profit to the industrial company without compensation.

2. The holding company pattern.

The difference between this pattern and the previous one is that the original enterprise is not abolished after breaking into component parts but becomes a general corporation—the holding company and an independent corporation. The main part is then reorganized into a stock company controlled by the general corporation. The auxiliary production units are also reorganized into an industrial company which becomes a subsidiary of the general corporation. The non-production and business organs are put temporarily under the control of the industrial company to be turned over to the local government when conditions are right. The former Ma'anshan Iron and Steel Company followed this pattern when it was transformed under the stock system.

The Ma'anshan Iron and Steel Company introduced the stock system in September 1992 with formal approval by the state. The steelmaking and rolling plants and auxiliary production units and research institutes under the former company were reorganized into a limited stock company which was then permitted to issue stock and have this stock listed on the exchanges in Shanghai, Shenzhen, and Hong Kong. The mines which produced raw materials for the steel plants, the docks, and the building and maintenance units under the former company were separated from the stock company and reorganized into an industrial company. The former Ma'anshan Iron and Steel Group Corporation remains as the general corporation (composed of the managerial departments of the former company) and controls the stock company, and the industrial company becomes its subsidiary. Its hospital and schools are under the auspices of the industrial company and will eventually be turned over to the local government.

The representative of the holders of the Chinese stock in the limited stock company is the Ma'anshan General Iron and Steel Corporation. Their relationship is that between company and stockholders, or that between the holding company and its subsidiary. The industrial company and the limited stock company are equal corporations. When the system was changed, the limited stock company undertook an agreement to give priority to the use of the services and products provided by the industrial company under conditions of retaining the same prices and quality.

These two patterns have many things in common, although the reorganizations were made in different ways.

First, their goals and general ideas for reform are basically the same. That is, the enterprises must join the international market and take part in market competition both at home and abroad. If they are to have a firm footing in this market competition, they must have a solid operation mechanism. They should not shoulder the heavy social burdens as they did in the past, but rather reorganize "all-inclusive" enterprises, "take meals in different canteens," set aside the capital with low profits, and raise the rate of capital profit to absorb investments from home and abroad. For example, if the Shanghai General Petrochemical Works did not exclude non-subject units but included all its former assets in the stock company, the capital profit would be

CHAPTER IV TRANSFORMATION UNDER A CORPORATE SYSTEM

only 2.5 percent; but internationally, the rate of capital profit in petrochemical companies is generally between 8 and 10 percent. If the capital profit rate is as low as 2.5 percent, it is very difficult to list these stocks on any exchange.

Second, after these enterprises have been reorganized, not only the stock companies set up efficient economic mechanisms, but the units separated from the stock company are forced to face the question of how to survive and grow in market competition. For example, the machinery plant under the former Shanghai General Petrochemical Works, after its separation from the parent body, introduced a contracted responsibility system, obliging its units to look to the market for business contracts. As a result, the plant has developed some new and marketable products like its sodium choroid manufacturing machinery, high-speed pumps, and energy-saving butterfly-type check valves for the market and is now determined to show a profit in one year.

Third, similar solutions have been found to the various problems arising from reorganization. In the introduction of the stock system there are generally two very difficult problems that arise. The first concerns losses suffered by the former enterprises and units which had provided services and products to the principal plants. The second is the question of survival of the enterprise's non-production units. These non-business units in the large state-owned enterprises such as the kindergartens, schools, hospitals and employee housing administration find it difficult to survive independently after reorganization because they are non-profitable units. Theoretically, the government administration should be separated from enterprise management when the enterprises are reorganized, and these non-profitable units should be turned over to the local governments. But the local governments do not have the funds to support these social service units.

The two problems described above may be solved through the industrial companies themselves.

Fourth, this form of agreement has been used in handling the relationship between the enterprise with its system changed, and the enterprise with its system unchanged (the stock company and the industrial company), namely, the stock company undertakes by agreement to give priority to the use of services provided by the enterprise separated from it under the condition of unchanged quality and prices.

Fifth, when the limited stock company sells stock to its employees it also treats the employees separated from it as though they were its own employees and sells the same amount of stock to them with, approval of the state.

In practical operation, because there is a holding company in the second pattern, it is useful to coordinate the relationship between the stock company and the industrial company; because after reorganization they have become different parts, independent of each other; but are still linked to each other. For example, they will want to use the infrastructure facilities of the former enterprise (roads, hotels, water and power supplies), and provide labor, services, and products to each other. As another example, the schools and hospitals are indispensable to the employees of all enterprises. Besides, public facilities must be maintained and constructed by all enterprises. All such relations will be best handled by the group corporation.

(IV) Some typical forms of corporate enterprises have emerged in the transformation of state-owned enterprises under the corporate system in China.

In China, experiments in the transformation of state-owned enterprises (or collective enterprises) under the corporate system began in the early 1980s, and experiments introducing the stock system were made on a wider scale after 1987. Of the above ways of reforming the property rights system, it should be said that the change to a property right structure with the stock company as its support most resembles a modern property rights system. Some typical forms of these corporate enterprises are described in the following pages:

1. Stock companies with state-owned stock and diversified investors as their main feature. The predecessor of the Shanghai No. 2 Textile Machinery Stock Co., Ltd was the Shanghai No. 2 Textile Machinery Plant, a large key enterprise in China's textile machinery industry. It was a typical state-owned enterprise before

CHAPTER IV TRANSFORMATION UNDER A CORPORATE SYSTEM

reform. Its production, supply and marketing were controlled by the Ministry of Textile Industry while its manpower, financial power and material power were under the leadership of the department in charge of the Shanghai Municipal Government. When reform began, the No. 2 Textile Machinery Plant explored ways to obtain decision-making power, resulting in a great change in the structure of state-owned property rights. But a strange phenomenon emerged in the course of the shift of these rights. On the one hand, the enterprise claimed greater power and rights from the government so that the managers would have relatively full property rights. On the other hand, as the sole representative of the enterprise's owner, the government had to take part in its major activities and business operations. In order to eliminate this anomaly there had to be an innovation in the system and a set of new rules of conduct established between the owner and the managers. Therefore, with approval of the Shanghai Municipal People's Government, the Shanghai No. 2 Textile Machinery Plant was reorganized into a limited stock company in December 1991. Today, it has a total of capital stock worth of 426 million yuan, including 46.31 percent in state-owned stocks, 1.57 percent in corporate stock, 11 percent in privately owned stock, and 41.12 percent in stock owned by foreign investment, forming a multi-owner capital stock structure with the state-owned stock as its largest constituent. Moreover, the new company has set up a revised system of leadership, policy making, and supervision comprising meetings of stockholders, the board of directors and the board of supervisors, thus ensuring that the rights and interests of the owners will not be infringed and the property rights of the enterprise protected.

In the course of reform the Shanghai No. 2 Textile Machinery Stock Co., Ltd, like the other stock companies transformed from former state-owned enterprises, faces the question of who will represent the state-owned stock. The general practice is that the position of representative for state-owned stock is left vacant temporarily or is represented by the government department in charge. Both practices have advantages and disadvantages. In order to safeguard the rights and interests of the state-owned stock and avoid new interference from the government department in charge, the meeting of the company's stockholders decided that the chairman of the board and general manager should represent the state-owned stock. Whether this practice is a good one or not must be tested by future practice.

2. Stock companies with state-owned corporations holding most of the stock. The Hengtong Real Estate Stock Co., Ltd in Zhuhai is a modern corporate enterprise initiated by 20 corporate bodies. The stock held by the first 10 large investors accounts for 82 percent of the company's subscribed capital. Except for two corporations of mixed ownership, all of the eight other investors are large and medium-sized state-owned enterprises. Under the company's regulations the meeting of the investors is the supreme organ of company power and is convened once a year. It has the power of "examining, approving and making decisions" relating to the distribution of profit, major appointments and dismissals, and changes in the capital stock. In relation to the company's development plan, production, business operation, budget and final accounting it has the power of "hearing and examining" only. Therefore, the state-owned enterprises investors, like other investors, are entitled only to the profit from the increased value of assets and take part in making major policy decisions only through the board of directors. They do not take part in day-to-day business operations. The company vests responsibility in the president (senior manager) under the leadership of the board of directors, which is also the permanent executive organ of the meeting of investors. The board of directors calls meetings twice a year. After these meetings the board of managing directors sets policies and makes decisions on major questions, and the managing directors inform each other of recent developments quarterly. The day-to-day business operations of the company are taken care of by the senior managers (i.e., president and vice-presidents), exercising full power. In the Hengtong Company the managers have the independent right to use assets and take part in making decisions affecting the transfer of company assets and the distribution of profit under the leadership of the board of directors (both the president and vice-president are directors, and the

CHAPTER IV TRANSFORMATION UNDER A CORPORATE SYSTEM

president is also concurrently the chairman of the board). In fact, the Hengtong Company possesses property rights over its assets as a modern corporation. It also provides stable guarantees of the managers' devotion to the business operations and development of the company.

Although under current conditions in China the legal procedure for untransformed state-owned enterprises to exercise the function as owners and invest state-owned assets in other enterprises has not yet been established, practice has shown that state-owned corporations holding stock in which some state-owned enterprises invest their "disposable assets" in other enterprises has formed a screen between the state and these enterprises, effectively separating state ownership from property rights. The state as the ultimate owner gets the owner's profit indirectly from the state-owned corporate stockholders, and neither the relevant government department (representative of the owner) nor the stockholders have the right to interfere with day-to-day business operations. Therefore, this form is a valuable attempt to overcome the malpractices existing within the traditional state-owned property rights system in China.

3. A state-owned enterprise at the county level has been transformed into a modern company. The Bao'an Enterprise (Group) Stock Co., Ltd was the first stock enterprise after China began economic reform. Its predecessor was a state-owned enterprise subordinate to the county government. The Bao'an County Joint Investment Company was formed in November 1982 by following the model of the stock system. In the beginning, the company issued stock certificates and paid with interest under company regulations. It organized as a stock cooperative enterprise for the purpose of raising funds. After years of development, its methods were gradually standardized. It was recognized by the Shenzhen Municipal People's Government as a limited liability company in September 1990. Now, it has become a large enterprise group of state-owned stock, corporate stock, and public stock with net assets of more than 2 billion yuan and subscribed assets totalling 3.5 billion yuan.

The history of the development of the Bao'an Group can be

said to be an epitome of the history of development of the stock company in China. From "buying stocks voluntarily and withdrawing investment freely" to "no withdrawal of investment, but allowance to buy, sell, give, inherit and mortgage stocks"; from "one investor, one vote" to "one vote for each share"; and from a small state-owned enterprise subordinate to the county government, to a large trans-industrial, trans-regional, and transnational stock company has been the Group's history. These step-by-step changes were totally free from the fetters binding traditional state-owned enterprises and established today's structure management.

4. The Zhongce phenomenon. The so-called "Zhongce phenomenon" refers to the Zhongce Investment Ltd in Hong Kong which in the last two years invested 2.5 billion RMB yuan and transformed 100 state-owned enterprises into Chinese-foreign joint ventures in a very short period of time. Since reform began, the use of capital funds, advanced equipment and managerial expertise from overseas to transform state-owned enterprises has spread, but the large-scale entry of one overseas company like Zhongce in some domestic industries or cities is still rare. It is indeed a phenomenon worthy of further study.

The differences between the "Zhongce phenomenon" and other Chinese-foreign joint ventures are: First, the Zhongce Investment Ltd with vast capital and rich experience in the financial operations obtained over 51 percent of the holding rights of the joint ventures in the form of cash investments; second, after the joint ventures were established, it totally transformed the operating mechanisms of the original state-owned enterprises; third, by using its holding rights in the joint ventures, it reorganized joint ventures listed overseas and reinvested newly raised capital funds in more state-owned enterprises on the mainland; fourth, as the targets for its direct investments, Zhongce chose either large and medium-sized state-owned enterprises with profits in industries, such as rubber, paper, and beer, or medium-sized and small state-owned enterprises in some cities, such as the Economic Commission system of Quanzhou and the light industrial systems of Ningbo and Dalian, to highlight the advantages

CHAPTER IV TRANSFORMATION UNDER A CORPORATE SYSTEM

of economies of scale.

The major point of the "Zhongce phenomenon" is that Zhongce Ltd holds 51 percent of the controlling stock in the joint ventures. This serves three purposes: It gains decision-making power in the joint ventures since the chairmen of the boards of directors of the joint ventures are appointed by the Zhongce Ltd; it also gains power over personnel; and through its 51 percent of controlling rights, it avoids domestic channels for approval. Therefore, it is not difficult to see that the real motive for Zhongce's massive entry into state-owned enterprises on the mainland lies in its use of the 51 percent of investments to gain 100 percent of controlling rights over the joint ventures.

The structure of property rights in the original state-owned enterprises which Zhongce Ltd now controls has itself undergone important changes. With dual subjects of the rights of ownership and power in the hands of Zhongce Ltd, the holder of these property rights has shifted from the original departments in charge of the enterprises to Zhongce Ltd. Although Zhongce Ltd appoints only one person as chairman of the board, and a member of the original management of the enterprise is the vice-chairman and concurrently general manager, the general manager is responsible to the board of directors and obeys its decisions. Among the directors, the representative of the state-owned assets and the representative of Zhongce Ltd have shown clearly different degrees of interest in the operations of the assets: The former is an agent entrusted by the government and the assets of the enterprises have no direct relationship to him personally, while the latter is the direct investor and attaches great importance to the operations of the joint ventures, playing a full role in decision making and supervision. Therefore, the imbalance of ownership rights and the risks and duties of the representative of the state-owned assets have enabled Zhongce Ltd to obtain the right to use, the right to profit from and the right to transfer 100 percent of the assets of the joint ventures. No wonder the factory directors and managers of the original state-owned enterprises regarded the joint ventures as enterprises of the Zhongce family after they were established.

Opinion varies on how to appraise the "Zhongce phenomenon." Our investigation shows, however, that one thing is certain: Because of asymmetrical dual ownership and property rights shifting from the government department in charge of the enterprises to the investors, people are beginning to show real interest in the use of enterprise assets, forcing enterprises to change their operating mechanisms and enabling state-owned enterprises to succeed after they become joint ventures. This has provided an important inspiration for reform of the state-owned enterprise system.

On the other hand, the "Zhongce phenomenon" is also likely to cause disputes. Because of inadequate preparations there were often crude, indiscriminate, and incomplete evaluations of assets. How the new industrial policies of the state will suit the market economy and absorb large-scale overseas investments remains to be seen. There is still a large gap between the current regulations for domestic market transactions, especially the rules of the capital market, and international practices. How to close this gap as soon as possible in order to guarantee the legitimate rights and interests of state-owned assets in joint ventures is a question that must be answered too. These are the new developments and new problems that have come with overseas capital controlling, buying or marketing shares in state-owned enterprises, and they certainly merit further study and exploration.

(V) Encouraging state-owned enterprises to adopt the shareholding system and deepening their reform.

1. Under the modern market economy the most important form of asset organization is the stock system.

(1) Companies emerged when participants in the market wanted to put themselves in a better position to compete. The limited liability company was found to be the most effective and successful form of organization in the course of developing these companies. Historically, it was exactly after the birth of these companies, especially stock companies, that capitalism entered its peak stage and created a powerful productive force in less than 100 years—a productive force stronger than the sum total of all

CHAPTER IV TRANSFORMATION UNDER A CORPORATE SYSTEM

productive forces before it. Western economists and jurists hold that the limited liability company is a great invention of this new era and that its importance is far greater than the steam engine and electricity. Without it, large-scale modern production was absolutely unimaginable.

(2) The share-holding system has the following characteristics:
—Limited liability
—Facility for raising funds
—Expansion of scale
—Stability of capital
—Transferability of stocks
—Separation of ownership from the right of operation
—Continued enterprise existence.

2. The stock system plays an important role in the reform of state-owned enterprises.

—The establishment of the operating system for state-owned assets calls for the adoption of the stock system. This system for state-owned assets under the market economy is established with the intermediate operation organs for state-owned assets as the core. The intermediate operation organs for state-owned assets, including holding companies and investment companies, operate in the form of the stock system so as to facilitate the absorption of other capital investments and the separation of the management of state-owned assets from their operation. The business enterprises organized with the investments from the holding companies and investment companies usually adopt the form of a stock system to help the medium organs make cross investments in the enterprises and shift the investments and adjust the investment structure at any time through the transfer of stock.

—The separation of government administration from enterprise management and the change of government functions call for the adoption of the stock system. An important measure to separate government administration from enterprise management is the application of the principle of an internal administration structure of the enterprise corporation to cut off direct administrative relations between government and enterprises. The most integrated and effective administrative structure is the limited liability company. We should establish enterprises of mixed ownership by encouraging capital to buy stocks so that the government departments cannot directly interfere with the enterprises and are forced to modify their functions.

—The reform of the property rights of enterprises calls for the adoption of the stock system. During the reform of the property rights of state-owned enterprises, small enterprises can directly transfer their property rights. However, there is a great degree of difficulty in transferring all property rights of the large and medium-sized enterprises. The most effective way is to transform the large and medium-sized enterprises under the stock system to fully circulate and transfer stocks and diversify property rights.

—To achieve optimum results from state-owned assets and shift state-owned assets from general industries and trades to basic industries, key fields, and public utilities, existing enterprises in the general competitive industries can be transformed under the stock system so they will gradually transfer their stock and exit the general fields of competition. The stock system may also be adopted even in basic industries, infrastructure facilities, and public utilities in order to absorb non-state capital investments in these fields. There are already successful precedents both at home and abroad.

3. Great importance should be attached to the transformation of state-owned enterprises under the stock system to push forward the development of state-owned enterprises in the direction of the stock system.

(1) In the transformation of state-owned enterprises under the corporate system, three forms are usually adopted, namely, the limited liability company, the limited liability stock company and the exclusive state-owned capital company. The exclusive state-owned capital company usually obtains in special economic fields. The limited liability company plays a limited role in the reform of state-owned enterprises because its stock cannot be easily transferred, the administrative structure of the legal entity is not strict, and the scale of the company is also limited. So, the

limited liability stock company turns out to be the most convenient and flexible form. It is most effective and achieves better results. Therefore, great importance should be attached to the stock system in enterprise reform. The stock system should be introduced with vigorous effort in the transformation of state-owned enterprises where conditions permit.

(2) Attention should also be paid to standardization when the stock system is being introduced. It is particularly necessary to standardize the behavior of the government as investors and managers so that the enterprises practicing the stock system can indeed operate effectively. In the course of experiments in introducing the stock system, the biggest problem has been that since the behavior of the government is not standardized, the enterprises with a stock system change only in form, but not in essence, and the role they should play is lost. Therefore, while introducing the stock system, this should be coupled with reform of the macroeconomic administration system so that changes can be truly effected.

II. The Chinese Style of the Western Modern Corporate System

(I) The study of reform of the enterprise system must proceed from the actual conditions in China.

To proceed from the actual conditions in China, we call the traditional enterprise system the planned economy, and the modern enterprise system the market economy. The theoretical basis for the planned economy is the theory of a product economy, and the system basis is the planned economy system. It refuses to recognize the commodity as commodity, money as money, price as price, or even enterprise as enterprise. By overconcentrated administration the state distorted the commodity economy into a product economy. The enterprise system of the market economy is the Chinese version of the Western modern corporate system. The theoretical basis for the Chinese enterprise system of the market economy is the theory of the socialist commodity economy, and its system basis is the socialist market economic system.

After 16 years of reform the enterprise system of the planned economy has been released preliminarily from the tight fetters of the planned economy system, and state-owned enterprises have passed from a rigid state of isolation from the market to a state of entry into the market with vigor. Although the vigor of state-owned enterprises is not yet sufficient, we cannot negate the results achieved in the first stage of reform in China. At present, the reform of the enterprise system in China has entered into the second stage, that is, making a further transition from the enterprise system of the planned economy to the enterprise system of the market economy—the modern enterprise system.

There are two questions that merit study: First, how to achieve the Chinese style of the Western modern corporate system and achieve unity of public ownership system and the corporate system; second, to make clear how many state-owned enterprises in China are ready to change from the enterprise system of the planned economy to the modern enterprise system in one step, and how many are not ready. What form of transition shall be used to change state-owned enterprises without these conditions for direct change to the modern enterprise system? This is a question that must be answered in reforming the state-owned enterprise system.

China is a socialist country and a developing country, but an unevenly developed country. These three basic characteristics dictate that reform in China must adhere to the principle of seeking truth from facts.

First, we should incorporate some feasibility experiences of the Western modern corporate system based on private ownership. But we cannot copy them indiscriminately. We must make the Western modern corporate system Chinese to achieve a unity of the corporate system and the system of public ownership.

Second, though we wish to make use of some Western experience, we cannot copy indiscriminately from the West because many conditions in our country differ from those in the developed Western countries.

Third, our state-owned enterprise system must be changed

CHAPTER IV TRANSFORMATION UNDER A CORPORATE SYSTEM

from the enterprise system of the planned economy to the enterprise system of the market economy—the modern enterprise system. This is the final goal of reform. However, we cannot seek a cure-all, nor can we "make it in one step." Appropriate forms of transition should be permitted in the light of varying conditions.

There are three categories of state-owned enterprises to which the modern enterprise system is not applicable:

The first category is the small state-owned enterprises which do not have the prerequisites for adopting a modern enterprise system. For example, many small state-owned industrial and commercial enterprises run by counties which should not have been turned into state-owned enterprises were, however, changed into state-owned enterprises in the course of transforming to private ownership. Some of them are small, locally run state-owned enterprises set up during the Great Leap Forward in 1958 and in the nationwide upsurge of agricultural support industries. These small state-owned enterprises should be changed from the state-owned economy to the cooperative economy. In transforming these enterprises, the cooperative pooling system has been introduced in most regions, namely, after evaluation of the assets of these enterprises, their employees obtained stock on a voluntary basis. Employees with financial difficulties were permitted to pay by installments. Such changes in the ownership system better suit the relation of production to the level of development of the productive forces, and better arouse the enthusiasm of employees. Results of these experiments have proved satisfactory in many regions.

Some small state-owned enterprises can be contracted out or leased for operation by the employees while retaining state ownership as the basic means of production. When conditions ripen, the state-owned economy can be transformed into the cooperative economy linked by the cooperative pooling system.

The second category includes state-owned enterprises producing special products or state-owned enterprises in special industries and trades such as the enterprises producing armaments and coins, and processing rare and precious metals, mineral resources, and highly sophisticated technologies. These state-owned enterprises shall continue under exclusive state ownership and the modern enterprise system of limited liability companies or limited liability stock companies is not applicable to them.

The third category includes very successful state-owned enterprises, which have both the conditions to attract investment and the capability to invest in other enterprises. However, among these particular state-owned enterprises, some believe that it is more profitable to expand their own production than for them to invest in other enterprises. Others believe it does not pay to take in investments and give part of their huge profits to other units in the form of dividends.

Except for the above three categories of state-owned enterprises, most of state-owned enterprises will be reorganized into limited liability companies in accordance with the requirements of the socialist market economic system. Those with ripe conditions shall be changed into limited stock companies, but only a minority of them shall be listed for sale. The national industrial corporations shall be gradually changed to holding companies, but one holding company won't be allowed to monopolize an entire industry or trade.

(II) China should study the modern corporate system in the West and consider how to make it Chinese.

The Western modern corporate system was the product of the development of capitalism under given conditions. During this period, private capital and its professional managers emerged. As a result, there was a division between the property owners and their agents and the socialized operations of private capital. This was called the "corporate revolution" in the West. Prior to this, the owners of capital exercised the right to manage the capital themselves. There was no question of entrusting the right of ownership, nor was there the division of labor between the property owners and agents. The "corporate revolution" brought about three changes in the property rights and managerial systems:

(1) It gave rise to the corporate system, the division between

CHAPTER IV TRANSFORMATION UNDER A CORPORATE SYSTEM

investors and the corporation, and the management of private capital;

(2) The owners of capital turned over the right to possess and use the property and the right of transfer to the corporate enterprise.

(3) The enterprise corporation can independently possess, control, use and dispose of the capital which they are entrusted to manage and the assets formed through the market, and assume civil responsibility as their assets. The capital owners assume only limited liability for their investments, and the creditors have the right to claim repayment of debts from the enterprises.

How can we make the Western modern corporate system Chinese? This question must be answered in the course of introducing the modern system.

It is essential to differentiate the public ownership corporate system from the private ownership corporate system: Under private ownership, the capital owners entrust their agents, namely the managing directors or managers to handle their capital. This is the managerial method of the Western modern corporate system.

In the public economy, the capital owners are the agents themselves. This differs from private enterprises in which the investors entrust ownership to the corporations which are the agents responsible for managing business operations and exercising the property rights of the corporation. Therefore, the public economy is an agent economy which calls for an even stronger check and balance mechanism, and for the division of power. The Western modern corporate system contains only two rights: The ownership of the investor and the ownership of the enterprise corporation. This does not conform to the needs of the public economy in China. Therefore, it is necessary to transform the Western system into a Chinese system.

The property rights and managerial systems are the principal component parts of modern enterprise. We can make use of the method of separating investors' rights of ownership from the property rights of the corporation as in the Western system, and replace private ownership with public ownership to achieve unity between the corporate system and public ownership. This is the first step toward making the Western corporate system a Chinese one.

The second step is to transform the managerial system of the West. Namely, by dividing that system into two levels: The first level is the property rights relation between the ownership of the investors and those of the corporation, namely the "entrusting —trustee" system existing between the investors and the board of directors. The second level is the property rights relation between the corporation and the managers in activating these rights, namely the system of "granting contracts—accepting contracts" between the board of directors and the general manger, the representative of corporate contracts, with the enterprise manager (the board of directors grants contracts) for the corporation. The manager fulfills the aim of preserving and increasing the value of state-owned assets and uses this as the basis for rewards and penalties. The advantages of these change are the establishment of dual check and balance mechanisms to strengthen checks by investors on the board of directors and to strengthen the checks and balances of the overall corporation. The purpose of using the dual checks and balances system is to enable the managers of enterprises to concentrate their power and responsibility and prevent inefficient operations from arising from decentralized power and responsibility.

To make the property rights and managerial systems of the West responsive to the needs of China we must achieve the combination of public ownership, the corporate system, the "entrusting—trustee" system and the system of "granting contracts —accepting contracts" simultaneously.

(III) Why do we need to practice the managerial systems of "entrusting—trustee" and "granting contracts—accepting contracts?"

Let's discuss the question by examining the Hengtong Real Estate Co., Ltd (hereafter called Hengtong) in the Zhuhai Special Economic Zone, Guangdong Province, as an individual case. Hengtong is a stock enterprise registered in August, 1991 with corporate public ownership as stockholders. Its registered capital was 18 million yuan (1,800 shares), subscribed by 20 initial investors. The first 10 shareholders hold 80 percent of the total, and eight of the first 10 are state-owned enterprises. The result of operations for 1992 and 1993 show that shares rose from 18 million yuan to 86.8 million yuan, and profits increased from 316,100 yuan to 54.3804 million yuan. These results are outstanding and demonstrate successful business development.

Hengtong combines public ownership with the corporate system. It shows that public ownership enterprises can adopt the corporate rights system suitable for conditions in China.

Can the board of directors of state-owned enterprises show close interest in preserving and increasing the value of their own property like corporate shareholders of private enterprises? Experience of Hengtong shows that the answer seems affirmative. Actually, it is not. An investigation discovered that Hengtong's results were not so much because of self-restraint on the part of the owners as from the hard work of the corporate administration —management headed by the general manager. The reason is that the property rights structure of Hengtong is different from that of modern companies in the West. Over 80 percent of Hengtong stock is held by the legal persons of public enterprises. By October 31, 1993, stock held by individuals in the company had accounted for only 16.6 percent of the total. In Western stock companies, capital stock is held by family members, a large number of private investors, and financial institutions that serve private investors. The difference between the public enterprise legal person stockholders and private stockholders in Western companies is that the former are the trustees of the investors while the latter are the investors themselves. Therefore, the binding force of the property rights mechanism is quite different.

How can we strengthen the entrusting party's control of the properties or the trustees of the properties—the board of directors and the general managers? It seems that the Western managerial system of "entrusting—trustee" alone is powerless. We can only find the solution by making the Western modern corporate system Chinese.

How can this be accomplished? The solution is to establish the dual check-and-balance mechanism, namely, to institute the "entrusting—trustee" system on the relations of property rights between the stockholders and the board of directors, and institute the system of "awarding contracts—accepting contracts" on the relations of property rights between the board of directors and the general manager. In other words, the board of directors is the party which gives the contract to the general manager for the management of corporate property rights conditionally, while the general manager who accepts the contract undertakes to fulfill the goal of preserving and increasing the value of the state-owned assets. This will give play to hard restraint in the check-and-balance contract mechanism.

This contract mechanism unifies the restriction mechanism and the stimulation mechanism. The stimulation mechanism is the interest-motivated mechanism, including both positive and negative stimulation. Contracting with every employee and at every level with work directly linked with personal material benefit can give full play to the initiative and creativity of the employees. This is an advantage distinctive to socialist state-owned enterprises. Moreover, the market economy is an economy under the rule by law, and contracts have legal effect and are a mandatory restraint. It has a much stronger binding force than the "entrusting—trustee" system.

To strengthen the binding force of the owners' property rights it is necessary to enact two more important measures:

The first is to practice multiple systems in one enterprise and strengthen the binding force of ownership. Since China allows the simultaneous development of multiple economic sectors with public ownership as the mainstay, it of course encourages the development of multiple systems of ownership in one enterprise by drawing investments from its employees or allowing the coexistence of multiple economic sectors in one enterprise with public ownership as the mainstay. This is not the "mixed economy." Property rights can be combined, but absolutely not mixed. Mixed property rights is the negation of property rights boundaries, which no social system permits. The laws of those countries practicing private ownership provide that private properties are sacred and inviolable while the laws of the countries practicing public ownership provide that publicly owned properties are sacred and inviolable. Either limited liability companies with state-owned corporations, the state holding the controlling shares, or the limited stock companies are allowed to seek private investment from both home and abroad. These investments cannot change the nature of the leading role of public ownership, but can strengthen mandatory restrictions on the investors' right of ownership.

The second measure is to practice the "golden rice bowl" salary system for senior managerial personnel. The salaries of senior managers shall be fully monetarized. Their wages, housing and cars shall all be included in the money salaries. The "golden rice bowl" system of high salaries shall be linked to achievement and the competition mechanism of the personnel market so that poor managers may be dismissed and replaced by more competent managers at any time.

III. Readjustment of the Enterprise Structure and Organization of Corporate Groups

(I) **The strategic readjustment of the industrial structure and product mix is an important factor in determining the economic growth rate and economic results. Readjustment of the industrial structure calls for a corresponding readjustment in the enterprise structure. The transformation of state-owned enterprises under the corporate system in China must be carried out in conjunction with this requirement.**

As everyone knows, there are many factors affecting the economic growth rate and economic results, such as new input for expanded production, the development of technologies, and the inclination of policies. When an analysis is made of the accumulation of assets alone, it is not difficult to see that strategic readjustment of the industrial structure and product mix is a very important factor.

To achieve a three dimensional integration of structure, growth rate, and results in the process of marketization the degree of adaptability of the product mix to consumers and the market, through structural adjustment, must be raised.

Therefore, the following principles should be followed:

1. Structural adjustment must be focused on the future, seeking compatibility with the modern international market and making use of comparative advantages to develop new industries. By adjusting inventory and increasing quantity, gradually rationalizing and optimizing the industrial structure, and finally attaining a high technological level with a product mix to meet the changing demands of the market, we can achieve strong competitive power and greater economic results.

2. The relationship between inventory and increased quantity should follow the principle of attaching equal importance to both. Part of the industrial structure will be improved through readjustments, but to reach the highest level it also will be necessary to increase quantity. Therefore, while readjusting the inventory of existing enterprises, we must readjust the increased quantity, strengthen the dynamics of the increased quantity and improve the irrational structure as soon as possible.

3. The relationship between key readjustments and general readjustments must be coordinated. General readjustments are the foundation and key readjustments are the core. Without the key point, there is no policy. Without a major breakthrough, it is difficult to open new prospects. As conditions vary from region to region, it is necessary to concentrate the proper forces on the readjustment of the key points in a purposeful and timely manner. Goals must be realistic, assignments must be definite, plans must be detailed, responsibility must be fixed, and a definite time limit must be set. They condition and promote each other, but also influence and restrict each other. Therefore, work must be done in a coordinated and systematic way.

4. Neither the readjustment of the growth rate nor the readjustment of results should be ignored. Because they compli-

ment each other, we must adhere to putting results first. Otherwise it will be impossible to improve the economic situation of enterprises and financial revenues; the development of these enterprises will be restricted and both national and local economies and revenues will be in unfavorable positions. To ensure that readjustments are made fruitfully, specific industries and products should be targeted as key points for readjustment. The current and future pillar industries should be taken as the key points with fixed technologies, grades, time limits, management, and guarantees. Only in this way can successful readjustments be made.

5. The relationship between structural readjustment and technological progress is a central concern. If structural readjustment aims at creating first-class enterprises and making first-class products, the key is technological progress. Technological progress can help develop and expand the pillar industries and help a number of state-owned enterprises, especially those of large and medium-sized, to increase their reserve strength for further development and raise their competitive power.

(II) Valuable inspiration from a comparative analysis of Chinese and Japanese enterprise groups.

The enterprise group is a form of organization integration among enterprises. According to the modern Western enterprise theory, the enterprise group is regarded as an intermediate organization between the market and enterprises. It has multiple functions and is widely applicable to different economic and enterprise systems. Therefore, the integration of enterprises and the emergence of enterprise groups at a given stage of industrial development are a phenomenon found in all countries.

The development of enterprise groups has a different and particular history in each country. Of course there has been a time lag between the development of Chinese and Japanese enterprise groups. In China the enterprise groups are still in their initial stage while in Japan they have existed for half a century and have matured. We must therefore not only compare their external forms, but readjust our vision to see the entire developments of these enterprise groups to discover organizational innovations in the course of their evolution.

1. The behavior main bodies of forming groups.

Economic entities in Japan are not governmental but rather the multitude of enterprises scattered among the people. In this sense, the economic activities of different enterprises depend on their own needs and possibilities, and the economic policies adopted by the government have no administrative binding force on enterprises.

With the restoration and development of its national economy after World War II, Japan faced the problem of a "dual structure" arising from the growing differences between large and small enterprises. Under the market economy, the Japanese government could not use its administrative power to "merge the small into the big" or effect "forced marriages," but had to solve the dual: Structure problem in a way suited to market forces. So Japan chose the system of contracting at different levels, forcing the small and medium-sized enterprises to catch up with large enterprises in terms of the technological and managerial levels. At that time Japan lagged behind the developed countries and was in the process of gaining on and overtaking them. The large enterprises wanted small and medium-sized enterprises to process auxiliary parts so that they could themselves concentrate on the development of key technologies and the production of major parts. They also wanted to make use of cheap labor of smaller enterprises to lower their production cost. By joining the production system of large enterprises the smaller ones were sure to secure orders from them for their own survival, along with guidance and support from large enterprises in technology, equipment, personnel, funds, and management. Serial production groups were formed with this arrangement as the basis. Through the enterprise groups and the specialized division of labor, the enterprises formed very close ties with each other on the one hand, while on the other, they were locked in very fierce competition. Large enterprises not only made use of the small and medium-sized enterprises with which they had contracts, but also used a multitude of temporary workers. The Toyota Co., Ltd of

CHAPTER IV TRANSFORMATION UNDER A CORPORATE SYSTEM

Japan produces fully two thirds as many vehicles as General Motors (GM) in the United States, but employs only one tenth the number of General Motors workers. The difference lies in the fact that GM produces all its own parts while Toyota depends on contracted specialized plants for its parts and then assembles them. It can thus be seen that the enterprise groups in Japan are the outcome of realistic choices suitable to the demands of accelerating scientific and technological progress and an expanding economic scale.

China is developing enterprise groups with a legacy from its traditional system. Different from the situation in Japan, the major entity forming these groups in China is, first of all, the government. However, governmental participation in forming enterprise groups has obvious drawbacks, namely, the rush to forced integration of enterprises under administrative mandates which the central government has repeatedly opposed is unavoidable. Moreover, because of the use of administrative power as the method of integration, once reform is deepened, the enterprises will have more decision-making power the original administrative power will disappear, and the enterprise groups will inevitably disintegrate. According to an investigation into the light industrial system, enterprises groups that have survived for more than five years account for only 12 percent of the total. There are similarities in other industries.

By analyzing the development of enterprise groups in China in the light of Japan's experience we can affirmatively state that in China the government is fully necessary as the first force driving the development of enterprise groups. However, this governmental initiative eventually should be turned over to the enterprises or excessive replacement of these enterprises by the government could lead to a return of the old system in the course of reform. The channel for cultivating enterprise behavior should be an acceleration of the reform of the economic system to truly achieve the separation of governmental functions from enterprise functions, giving the enterprises full decision-making power so they can participate in the formation of enterprise groups compatible with the inherent features and requirements of their own development.

2. The key points of the central government's operation.

The role of the government should not be ignored in solving those particular questions which cannot be solved by enterprises by merely depending on their own forces because the market level is low in developing countries and there exists large gap between them and the advanced technological level abroad. The key to effective government assistance to the groups lies in the choice of conditions and methods of operation.

The Japanese government also intervenes in the macroeconomic activities of group enterprises. But this intervention is not direct participation in business operations, but is done to standardize the activities of the enterprises through a series of laws and policies. In encouraging the formation of enterprise groups the government of Japan follows practical and flexible industrial policies in the light of changing national conditions and economic development to establish a realistic foundation for the formation of these groups. In the 1950s, for example, Japan enacted special industrial development laws to improve the production level of new industries and prevent excessive competition. This brought about integration and mergers among enterprises and established the large-scale production systems formed from a number of small enterprises. In the 1960s the Japanese government set requirements for industrial reorganization and advocated effective competition by its enterprises in the international arena, with the goal of establishing an oligopoly. In its economic and social development plan of 1967, Japan stressed the oligopolistic system, practiced liberalism in relations with other countries, and followed a policy of forming giant enterprises at home. This fostered a number of large international enterprises. As for small and medium-sized enterprises, the Japanese government encouraged an appropriate production scale and the concentration and mergence of enterprises through incentives. Many of these small and medium-sized enterprises formed vertical production groups with large enterprises as their centers, thus combining the strength of large, medium-sized and small enterprises on the basis of advision of labor and coordination. Within the framework of large enter-

CHAPTER IV TRANSFORMATION UNDER A CORPORATE SYSTEM

prise groups, operations are constantly upgraded in the direction of technological development while at the same time they continue to weave themselves into a vertical and interlocking enterprise structure.

In the course of economic reform in China, especially while market elements remain imperfect, a long process is required for organizing enterprises into groups. The practical and immediate significance of the government's impulse is to help accelerate the growth of these groups during the progressive development of reform. The Chinese government, after serious study and exploration, has proposed the development orientation, organizational structure, and basic requirements for the formation of groups. But technical questions remain to be answered. In general, Chinese enterprises are underdeveloped, small, and uneconomical in scale. These characteristics of course are related to the history of their growth. This history has been one without competition and lacking market experience. Moreover, large and medium-sized state-owned enterprises have no power to make decisions affecting business operations and cannot make timely and correct response to changing social demands and economic realities. These large enterprises do have some economic and technological advantages, but at the same time are hampered by the many disadvantageous aspects of the system. Small enterprises, on the other hand, have freedom in business operations are saddled with but economic and technological disadvantages.

Drawing from the Japanese experience we can see that the Chinese government should not be hasty in linking enterprises into groups, but should first begin basic preparations for the formation of enterprise groups and solve the technical difficulties arising in such alliances. For example, at the Chongqing Automobile Group where the state is now making just such an experiment, the problem is the distance between two cooperative enterprises is too long, thus affecting the cohesive force of the group. According to the decision made by the Chongqing Automobile Group, the front axle of Steyr cars are produced at the Jinan Automobile Plant while the rear axle are produced at Dazu City in Sichuan Province and then the two plants will exchange for the final assembly. One-way transportation covers 2,500 kilometers. Such long-distance cooperation for the production of parts increases the transport cost which accounts for 10 percent of the total cost of an automobile, and the untimely supply of parts often affects normal production. This makes it difficult for the group to achieve relatively stable and efficient internal coordination.

3. The market system as medium.

The market economy demands the concentration of production and assets and the intensive use of production elements. The formation of an environment suitable for the market economy requires enterprise groups to constantly readjust their industrial structure and the structure of the enterprise organization in accordance with market demands. They must also make reasonable allocations of assets and readjust the inventory structure.

Japan is now a country practicing the market economy. We have seen that Japan used organization to make up for market shortcomings and did much of its business utilizing enterprise groups in the early stages of its economic development. However, all this was done, from the start, through the multiple employment of mergers, alliances, and divisions in accordance with market parameters. The characteristic industrial organizational policies in Japan are built on the basis of the modern market economy. Unlike many developed countries, Japan has incorporated a great deal of governmental will, policy, planning, and guidance into their economy, but the fundamental laws of the market economy still prevail. Governmental intervention is made largely through intervention in the market. The operation of the Japanese government appears simple and easy, and gets clear results. Therefore, only in the market economy can enterprises become the main bodies of behavior, with the market as the medium for ties among enterprises. The pattern of the market is changing day by day towards unity and synthesis, and is constantly creating changing alliances among enterprises.

Today, the market system in China is still imperfect. Large numbers of enterprises have not yet become the main bodies of behavior in independent business operations and have not yet

CHAPTER IV TRANSFORMATION UNDER A CORPORATE SYSTEM

acquired sufficient independence. Also, price forming and competitive mechanisms are not yet perfected. All this has forced the Chinese government to use more administrative means in the development of industrial groups.

As every system has its own internal driving factors, China must be able to absorb the cost factors arising from changes in the system and end various distortions caused by the policies of the government in the course of establishing the socialist market system. In other words, internal structures are needed to replace the old system, and this will take time and the readjustment of resources. Reform of the economic system in China is being pushed forward with a complete set of reforms and in a progressive way in many fields but is not yet able to provide the conditions for a smooth formation of enterprise groups. The formation of groups in China must proceed step by step. This is a restrictive condition which did not apply to the formation of groups in Japan. Therefore, the fruits of development of these groups in China depend on accelerating the development of the market and on promoting the coordination of social and economic relations.

4. Conditions for the choice of organizational structure.

Enterprise groups are formed to keep pace with the development of the national economy. It demonstrates historical precedents, but does not always follow the same pattern. A general theory of histology states that in static conditions a given structure of organization determines the function of that organization, and in the dynamic state the operation of the organization determines the performance of the functions.

In the course of forming enterprise groups, Japan has generally adopted two types of organizational structure. One is the financial group of several large enterprises with financial capital as its center and comprehensive corporations as the leaders. This structure was based on the groups formed by the pre-war monopoly tycoons and again developed in the course of Japan's economic reconstruction. Its unique organizational feature is a structure of circles within circles in which there is no one central industry. It is a large, loose association based on the circular ownership of stocks by its members, coordinated by a board of directors. The other type is the industrial group of enterprises formed by the contracting system with the industries as their center, closely related to the establishment and development of large enterprise systems. The characteristic of this organizational structure is the pyramid, with the giant company at the top, linked to a large number of medium-sized and small enterprises through business relations. These financial groups have a long history and carry out their multi-level business operations depending on certain financial conditions and the functions of the comprehensive companies. Industrial groups reflect the characteristic features of the concentration of modern enterprises and achieve a high degree of integration of technologies and production, calling for ever greater specialized division of labor.

The developing groups in China require the formation of a closely knitted organization receiving support from large industrial enterprises, and has the characteristic features of the second type of group organization in Japan. But in business operation they call for a multi-level operation and therefore have the function of the first type of Japanese groups. Comparing the conditions and operational methods of the two types of groups in Japan, we should address the questions of creating mixed operations and preparing practical conditions for the development of groups in China.

The situation in China is that specialized division of labor is not as developed as in Japan, and the banking system has not yet been channeled into the enterprise's business operations. This is perhaps because the Chinese groups have restrictions on their form of organization which are different from Japan. Therefore, most successful enterprise groups at present have the technical capability of multi-product industries. Without this capacity it is difficult for industries to form groups. China's late advantage is that enterprises can be organized directly at the very start of an economy of scale, and we can choose and create by comparing the advantages of various successful international groups. But an important question is how to positively create the conditions needed to develop these groups while promoting the rapid growth

CHAPTER IV TRANSFORMATION UNDER A CORPORATE SYSTEM

of the existing groups. It is first necessary to raise the organizational ability of the existing groups. Current financial companies are simply a transitional form with banking functions. An extension of the decision-making power over imports and exports can be regarded as the starting point for fostering enterprise groups. A problem for future solution is that in establishing the market economic system, these functions vital to the future development of the groups must be constantly enlarged.

5. The basic functions of contact links.

An enterprise group is a multi-functional community of interests with a multi-level organizational structure, and a method of contact must be established among its members. Its role is to strengthen the centripetal force of the group so that it will develop rationality.

It can be seen from the formation of groups in Japan that the integration of capital is of decisive importance to the birth of these economic groups. In the course of expansion, especially as the development of the group changes to suit the demands of economic growth, technical and professional contacts are the basis for accumulating group enterprise members. The characteristic feature of the integration of capital among Japanese enterprises is the way stock is held by corporations. The original ties of family monopoly among enterprises were broken with the dissolution of the financial magnates after the World War II, and new types of relationships among enterprises had to be built on the new basis. Japan chose a quick and convenient way through corporate stock ownership to stabilize business relations among the enterprises. Corporations hold stock generally in two ways: The matrix type of circular ownership of stock, and the radiating type of mutual stock ownership. These methods suit the growth of the two types of groups. After this, the transformation and integration of capital was complete. When this basic pattern for enterprise groups became stable and the development of stockholders from among the corporations became stagnant, group development turned toward cooperation and contracts in technology, information, and business. In essence, this further sought to rationalize the development of industrial groups.

Among the Japanese industrial groups, when legal persons held the stocks to form the group cores, corresponding groups could be formed more smoothly under their umbrellas. This was because the diversified business operations of enterprises in Japan were not developed, and large enterprises universally practice longitudinal division of business to increase trade among the enterprises. Trade between enterprises was done one on one, and became the standard practice and both cause and effect for the integration of enterprises. China does not have such an organizational background. In establishing internal relations in the enterprise groups in China, it is essential to solve simultaneously the problem of forming group cores and the problem of constructing reasonable production and business operating systems among the group members. In other words, there is a lack of market-type production and business systems, as well as the lack of a link for integrating assets in the internal relations of Chinese enterprise groups. The Japanese experience shows that the former is the basis for the formation of groups and the latter is the basic condition for the development of those groups.

Nuclear enterprises within Chinese enterprise groups are generally small in size and have little capital for reinvestment. Obviously, it is difficult for such nuclear enterprises to become the links needed for strengthening ties among the member enterprises. In order to reduce the time needed for market development the government is now experimenting with direct participation in connecting the assets of the industrial group companies. This includes authorization for the management of state-owned assets under the central government, the administrative transfer of state-owned assets within the limits of a region, and the reorganization of the stock companies. Whether this experiment will be successful or not depends on at least two factors. The first is the government's correct selection of the nuclear enterprises for combination in the light of internal technological and economic ties and their corresponding coordination. The second is to make certain that the production and business operating systems within the groups are adaptable to the market. It seems that at present there is a great degree of difficulty in this work. The Japanese

CHAPTER IV TRANSFORMATION UNDER A CORPORATE SYSTEM

enterprises have formed mature systems after many years of market experience. In China, the methods developed in Japan cannot be easily transplanted. The process of construction will depend on deepening reform of the economic system, the perfection of the enterprise's business procedures, and the creation of self-regulation mechanisms of industrial groups.

6. The significance of stressing effective competition.

The high-quality economic development is achieved through competition. There are many factors explaining rapid economic growth in Japan, but the driving force is competition. The development of enterprise groups in Japan has raised the degree of concentration of industries, accelerated the accumulation of capital, and led to monopolies in technological innovation and foreign trade. Whether in capital growth, profit rates, scale and capacity of production, or research, development, information dissemination, and foreign investment, the strength and influence of the groups far exceed that of large and medium-sized enterprises. Indeed, they have become true giants and now control the Japanese economy. However, the development of these groups has not strangled market competitions. Rather, economic development with the groups in the vanguard have kept creating new space for the survival of many enterprises and formed the pattern of competition at all levels of Japanese society. So far as competition related to the groups is concerned, there is monopoly competition among the different groups, selective competition between enterprises inside and outside of the groups, and internal competition arising from changes in the internal organization of the groups. All this shows that the groups themselves are characterized by the dual existence of monopoly and competition. The history of the development of enterprise groups in Japan has shown that the merging, combination, serialization and grouping of Japanese enterprises counterbalance an anti-monopoly policy. The policy of industrial development has a bearing on the merging and integration of enterprises, and has changed the small scale and low productivity of enterprises by preventing excessive competition. This demonstrates the greater success of the Japanese government in adopting flexible policies designed to engender effective competition.

There has never been a push for effective competition in the development and grouping of enterprises in China. In the actual market conditions of China a high degree of monopoly and excessive competition coexist. This is an obstacle to the formation of groups as well as the cause of the low quality within groups. As the economic scale of China's enterprise groups is relatively small, and since they possess only a low percentage of the market, their ability to gain economic monopoly is weak. A high degree of monopoly comes mainly from administrative functions, including the administrative functions of some industrial groups. The non-separation of government administration from enterprise management has enabled some groups to have a privileged position in some industries formed through administrative and market division. Because of this administrative monopoly, normal competition has difficulty overstepping the barriers created by this monopoly and cannot be carried on widely throughout society. Moreover, there is a lot of chaotic and unlawful competition which, to put it mildly, we call excessive competition. Therefore, many of the problems which must be solved in the current Chinese economy are actually ultra-economic or administrative problems manifested in economic form. Therefore, the reestablishment of the competitive structure of enterprises is an important task for the Chinese government to create space for the development of enterprise groups. This includes many arduous tasks, such as the selection of a market structure, expansion of market scope, establishment and unification of a standard market system, and the establishment and perfection of corresponding laws and regulations.

(III) Analysis of examples in founding corporate groups with property rights relations as the link.

The Nantong Machine Tools Stock Co., Ltd was set up in 1988. It is the first large enterprise group with the limited stock company as its core in Nantong, and was established on the pattern of the stock system under the condition of remaining part of the system of public ownership. The company group has

CHAPTER IV TRANSFORMATION UNDER A CORPORATE SYSTEM

adhered to the orientation of the international market by exporting its famous-brand milling machines and developing high-tech products, and has successfully applied the operational mechanism of the stock system to the change of business operations of state-owned enterprises. It also did a lot of exploration and practical experiments in optimizing enterprise organization, developing a large-scale economy adjusting its product mix, extending its business scope, accelerating scientific and technological advances and perfecting group management.

1. The transformation of the stock system.

The main enterprise of the company group—the Nantong Machine Tools Plant, a large, key enterprise under the Ministry of Machine-Building Industry, produces various types of milling machines. It is a second-class national enterprise, one of the enterprises designed for the export of machine tools, and a new- and high-tech enterprise in Jiangsu Province. With the development of the international market, the export volume of its machine tools has increased rapidly, with an annul growth rate of 50 percent for three consecutive years. Even so, it was still far from meeting export demand. The original pattern of integrated business operation of the enterprise—the Nantong Machine Tools Company embraced 15 other enterprises in the city, suburbs and rural counties—failed to form the core held together by their assets and shared risks because of the hindrance by the channel for the turning over of the revenues and relations of subordination. As a result, the enterprises in the group "ate together at the same table" but "cooked meals separately by themselves." The company group was unable to allocate production elements, carry out a unified plan, technical transformation, business operation and credits in accordance with market orientation, and found it difficult to form a large-scale economy.

To solve these problems it was essential to change the existing system from the pattern of cooperation by contract to the pattern of integration of assets. For this purpose, the Nantong Machine Tools Plant was transformed into a stock company in four steps, beginning in May 1988.

In the first step it used the relations of the right of business operations as the opening to create conditions for the merging of assets.

(1) Contracting with the legal person for the transfer of the right of business operation. The Nantong Machine Tools Plant contracted for management of a state-owned heat treatment plant and unified representation of the corporation so that the main plant obtained the legal right to operate, manage and profit for the length of the contract.

(2) Controlling creditor's rights and unifying the right of business operations. With creditor's rights as the fulcrum, the Nantong Machine Tools Plant obtained the right to make appointments and dismissals and the right of business operations in nine collective enterprises in the city, suburbs and rural counties for the scattered production of machine parts under one name, supervising the technological processes and quality control, and basically forming the embryo of the group for the unified right to operate the business. This created conditions for the reorganization of property rights and the integration of assets.

For the second step, it used the relations of property rights as the basis for building the group core of the structure of stock ownership.

Relying on main enterprises, the parent company is composed of nine enterprises, i.e., the Nantong Machine Tools Plant, the No. 3 Machine Tools Plant, the No. 4 Machine Tools Plant, the Heat Treatment Gear Plant, the Foundry Works, the Forging Plant, the Accessories Plant, the Casting Molds Plant, and the Motor Repairs Plant, with integrated assets and business operations. Registered common stock was issued to individuals and companies with a total worth of 1.65 million RMB yuan. Now, the company's assets total 53.5 million yuan composed of stock of equal value, the face value of each stock being 1 yuan, 53.5 million shares in total. The stockholders are divided into three categories according to the nature of the property ownership: State-owned stocks, 79.2 percent; corporate stocks, 17.1 percent; and individual stocks, 3.7 percent. The parent company practices unified cost accounting, tax payment, credit, profit and loss, and the integrated management of production, supply, and marketing.

CHAPTER IV TRANSFORMATION UNDER A CORPORATE SYSTEM

In the third step the Nantong Plant attracted investments and held the controlling stock as a way to establish an enterprise group with the stock company as its core.

(1) By using the joint ventures to hold the controlling stock, the company organized five Sino-foreign joint ventures—the U. S. Nantong Machine Tools Repairs Company, the Nantong Yandong Foundry Co., Ltd, the Weite Mechanism Co., Ltd, the Duofu Machinery Co., Ltd, and the Zhuyou Decorations Co., Ltd to form the nucleus of the group connected by production and business operations, with the stock companies holding the controlling stock.

(2) Among the related enterprises with investments in the group, it organized the four joint ventures holding group stock or having investments in the group, including the Nantong Yueli Plastic Products Co., Ltd, the Zhaoyuan Metal Structural Parts Co., Ltd, the Kandi Machinery Co., Ltd and the Shenzhen Saimu Machinery Co., Ltd to form the semi-nucleus for the coordinated production of parts.

For the fourth step the company increased its assets by issuing stock to become a listed company, with the aim of standardizing the operation.

In accordance with the standard requirements of the stock system, it established a modern enterprise organization including the meeting of stockholders, the responsibility of the general manager under the leadership of the board of directors to form a pattern of orderly operations, with power divided among the meeting of stockholders, the board of directors and managers, and the board of supervisors representing the rights and interests of the stockholders. Moreover, with the approval of the Organizational Department of the Nantong Municipal Committee of the Chinese Communist Party, it set up the CPC Committee of the Nantong Machine Tools Stock Co., Ltd, and with the approval of the Nantong Municipal Trade Union Council, established the Trade Union. Since this transformation the company has been recognized by the State Commission for Restructuring the Economy as a standardized stock company. With the approval of the People's Government of the Jiangsu Province, and the consent of the China Securities Regulatory Commission it issued 20 million RMB yuan of public stock in 1994, and its capital stock structure reaching the standards for a listed company, it is now listed on the Shanghai Stock Exchange. By these stages, the nuclear enterprise of the group became the first standardized listed company in Nantong.

2. The change in the stock system furthered the establishment of the modern enterprise system.

The company group carried out its transformation of the stock system at a time when the new system was superseding the old, but external conditions were still not complete and policies and laws were yet imperfect. Under these circumstances, the Nantong Municipal Commission for Restructuring the Economic Systems, the Municipal Economic Commission, the Municipal Bureau of Finance, the People's Bank, and 15 other municipal government departments discussed, coordinated, and worked out a dozen measures for readjustment. They were able to solve the difficult problems of taxation, credit, distribution of profit, labor, wages, assessments, and statistics, and push the establishment of the modern enterprise system through to standardized transformation.

The company straightened out relations between the centralization and decentralization of power to increase its cohesive force.

The company group is a stock company with public ownership as its basis. Many new problems soon began to appear in business operations and management. The member factories forming the nucleus of the group are independent enterprises without corporate status, but they are different sub-factories. Considering that the company represents the entire enterprise, and that it must be responsible to the state, society and investors, it must make full use of the advantages of the integration and properly concentrate business operations. But the factories at the core are scattered and form independent systems. In order to encourage them to directly organize production and play a dynamic role in fulfilling their assignments, the group adopted the system of "centralized leadership and classified management,"

CHAPTER IV TRANSFORMATION UNDER A CORPORATE SYSTEM

combining centralization and decentralization and forming a three-level management system on the basis of functions and responsibilities.

The meeting of stockholders is the group's supreme organ of power, representing the rights and interests of all stockholders and exercising ownership of the investors. The board of directors elected at the meeting of stockholders is the supreme policy-making organ in business operations. The group practices the system of group general manager responsibility under the leadership of the board of directors, and the general manager is wholly responsible for the production management and administration of the company. The plant directors at the nuclear level are authorized by the general manager to take charge of plant organization and administration, thus establishing a three-level management pattern at the strategic decision making level with the chairman of the board at the center, the business management level headed by the general manager, and the plant directors responsible at the production level. The group's headquarters is the investment decision-making and profit center. It has the power to make overall decisions, direct strategical development, and assume chief responsibility for planning in the future. The plants are the centers of production and processing, and organize day-to-day production activities under the unified plan and leadership of the company group.

(2) The group optimized the structure of the enterprise and organized the integrated entities for the management of assets.

The company group, organized with its assets as the link, broke away from the old pattern of single state ownership and formed an integrated enterprise coexisting with state-owned, collective, and individual assets. By practicing an integrated operation of assets, the company has separated ownership of the diversified investors from the incorporated property rights. The nine nuclear enterprises in the group were all machine builders producing parts for one another to form finished products through coordination. When they became represented by one corporation the old relations of coordination were changed from external circulating through the market to internal circulation under one unified command.

In accordance with market demands, the group has made internal adjustment to the production elements. On the one hand, it has concentrated its forces on intensive and precision processing to raise the technical level of its products and achieve longitudinal integration of production management. On the other, it gave full play to the advantages of their specialized division of labor and coordination to produce the various parts, forming eight manufacturing centers for transmission cases, gears, lead screws, main axles, tools, and machine maintenance. On the basis of the division of labor in the technical processes, they have formed six processing centers: Casting, forging, heat treatment, special and general metal cutting, and machine-tool assembly, achieving latitudinal integration for the development of a scale economy and raising the percentage of their market share.

(3) The product mix was readjusted and the scope of business operations expanded.

When the company was first established, the production of digital-controlled milling machines and processing centers were also in their infancy in China. There was a great demand for these products and the main center for producing ordinary lathes for the international market was shifting from the "four small dragons" of Asia (Hong Kong, Taiwan, Singapore and the Republic of Korea) to China. The group made the correct judgment for investment and concentrated its manpower and financial resources on the development of more than a dozen types of high-grade products. In 1994, orders for lathes exceeded 1,000. The main products at the stock-controlling level were more than 20 kinds of milling machines of various quality grades.

With this strong and comprehensive economic foundation, the company group was awarded a contract from the Nantong Heat Treatment Plant. As operations proved successful during the length of the contracted, the Bureau of Finance and the Bureau of Machinery decided to invest in the plant's more than 2 million yuan of state-owned assets in the company's nuclear projects as state-owned stock to become a subsidiary of the parent company. Exercising its function as the investment center, it has

CHAPTER IV TRANSFORMATION UNDER A CORPORATE SYSTEM

now invested 33.7 million yuan on the joint development of the vortex-type air conditioner compressor. With scientific research institutes. This is a sophisticated product incorporating the latest technology. When it is put into production, the company will have the capacity to produce 50,000 compressors annually. Another group joint venture, the Zhuyou Decorations Co., Ltd with an investment of US$700,000 will produce bamboo floor and wall boards, with an annual capacity of manufacturing 100,000 square meters. Nantong Yueli Plastics Products Co., Ltd, a joint venture with an investment of half US$500,000, will have an annual capacity of 1.8 million products.

3. The change in the stock system has brought about a totally new operations system.

In the past few years, the company group has greatly optimized enterprise organization and adjusted the industrial structure through the standard transformation to the stock system and the open issuance of its stocks to the public.

(1) As a step in its self-development, the company group has formed a structure for dividing its after-taxes profit into public accumulation funds, public welfare funds, and dividends in reasonable proportions. If the percentage of the public accumulation funds is too small, it will decrease investment in enlarged reproduction, thus affecting the investors' earnings. If it is too large, the dividends will be reduced and the investors' interests are harmed. Therefore, the proportions of the accumulation funds, welfare funds, and dividends must be standardized and appropriate to ensure the sufficient accumulation of funds for self-development and proper dividends for distribution among the investors, thus forming a distribution mechanism enabling self-development.

(2) The group is restrained by its investors, the independent law, and accounting offices, and public opinion by using the stock system and issuing stock to the public. So the investors keep a close eye on the management and development of the enterprise. The company receives more than 1,000 proposals from their investors every year and most of them are adopted. Apart from submitting financial reports to be relevant bureau in charge, the

company also submits statements of assets and liabilities, losses and profit, and changes in the financial situation to the authorized accounting and auditing offices for examination, thus perfecting the self-restraint mechanism.

(3) Considering independent operations, the company group practices the general manager responsibility system under the leadership of the board of directors. The board of directors is a permanent body and performs its duties in accordance with the Company Law, company's regulations, and the decisions made at the meeting of the investors. The board of directors appoints the general manager, the deputy general manager, and the chief accountant, examines the development plan and annual production and business operations plan, and makes decisions on the development of products to keep pace with market changes. In this way, the company group has changed from direct administration by the department in charge to indirect economic guidance through the relations of assets and investors exercising their power, thus acquiring full power to make independent business decisions. In the five years since it was established, it has developed 38 new products, earned a total of more than US$50 million in foreign exchange, and made a profit of 60 million yuan.

(4) Thanks to the adoption of the policy of assuming sole responsibility for its profits or losses, the company group has achieved good economic returns.

The Nantong Machine Tools Stock Co., Ltd (group) is now the embryo of a transnational enterprise. General ideas for its future development are to accelerate technological progress, develop transnational business operations, set up two large production bases for machine tools and air conditioner compressors, and set up sales companies in North America and Southeast Asia. The company already has set up six processing bases for casting, forging, heat treatment, special metal processing, die making and accessories production. By making full use of equipment, funds, personnel, and scale advantages it has developed a main industry with diversity, achieved the integration of scientific research, industrial production, and trade, and is marching toward a high-tech, export-oriented, and multi-functional transnational enter-

CHAPTER IV TRANSFORMATION UNDER A CORPORATE SYSTEM

prise group.

(IV) Developing a number of large transnational enterprise groups. We may use the Hualin Group as an example in the discussion of establishing transnational enterprise groups for international competition.

The predecessor of the Hualin Group was the state-owned No. 1 Rubber Plant, first built in Shenyang in 1938 and moved to Mudanjiang City in Heilongjiang Province in 1950. It now employs more than 10,000 people, with assets of 500 million yuan. As one of the largest rubber tire producing centers in China, it produced 1.8 million rubber tires and had sales of 1.1 billion yuan in 1993.

Transformation and reform are the characteristic features of the Hualin Group. In the past few years they have taken positive steps to find a good operational mechanism for the development of the enterprise. In 1993, the Hualin Group was formed with the Hualin Rubber Plant as its core and 10 other enterprises inside and outside the province as participating members. It introduced, on an experimental basis, the group management pattern characterized by its method of integration. In the same year it organized the Hualin Stock Co., Ltd, thus laying the foundation for the introduction of the modern enterprise system. While continuing to deepen reform of its labor and wage system, it separated 2,600 employees and 21 attached enterprises from the stock company and established a general social corporation in 1994. It is planned that their dependence on the group's economy will come to an end after the three-year transition.

The industrial structure of the Hualin Group is also changing. It is developing a diversified economy, and has extended its business to other countries. It has established or is establishing a tire retreading factory, a rubber machinery processing plant, and a building and transport enterprise, and is engaging in foreign, domestic, and border trade, opening the Xinyuan Company in Vladivostok. Substantial progress has also been made in setting up a joint tire-producing venture with Hong Kong investment.

The group also has invested in the building of a rubber processing mill in Thailand.

One question is how to handle relations between the absorption of capital and independent development. The policy-makers of the Hualin Group hold that their group is a large state-owned key enterprise, so they must be active in drawing investment from overseas on the one hand and avoiding control of the stock by overseas businessmen on the other. They have tried their best to get state support for the rapid development of the industry and to finally establish a management pattern superior to that of the joint venture.

Another question is how to handle the contradictions in a changing system which will create greater unemployment and less social stability. The Hualin Group is also faced with the problem of overstuffing. To solve it, they have provided new jobs or offered retraining to their laid-off staff and workers, and have chosen the best trained for other jobs that suit them best.

It is possible for the Hualin Group to become the first transnational company in China. This is because they have a good number of specialists rated among the best in China, have strong scientific and technical forces, and have imported the most up-to-date tire-producing technologies and equipment from Italy, France, and Japan. They also have kept up with new developments in the tire industry worldwide, including scientific and technical and market information. Hualin also is linked with the international pipeline in the import of raw and processed materials and exporting its own products. This is the objective condition. The subjective condition is that the representative of the corporation and the policy makers are farsighted and have the ambition to develop the national tire industry. They have clearly set the goal of "standing at the height of the world, walking in the frontline of reform, and building Hualin into a transnational group with great strength by the integration of scientific research, industrial production, and trade and banking." Practical development programs and a plan for their implementation have been worked out.

The state should adopt powerful measures to help large

enterprises like the Hualin Group become transnational groups as soon as possible. Because in the first place, the economies of the world are now approaching and mixing with each other, and larger exchanges and economic supplementation are irreversible courses. In the second place, for real development China's economy must face the world and take part in international competition. Third, the world market is very large and its demands are also large. In the face of diversified market demands, Chinese enterprises are sure to find ample scope for their abilities. What is said above is the general principle. Concretely speaking, the Chinese economy must be vigorously developed and exert more influence in the world. The Republic of Korea has for the last several decades devoted itself to the development of influential large enterprises and transnational companies which have played an important role in the steady development of its economy. Its experience is worth learning. It can be said that without a number of transnational companies, the country's economy cannot mature.

IV. Standard Operation of State-Owned Stocks and Standardization of the Corporate System

(I) **Changing state-owned enterprises to the stock system is the most effective measure for clearly defining the property rights of these enterprises. Great importance should be attached to the significant role of the reform of the enterprise's property rights.**

The economic practices of the international market demonstrate that the stock company is the most effective and successful form of organization for the process of development. The experiments with the stock system in China have also shown that the introduction of this system is conducive to the clear defining of property rights, the independence of an enterprise's property rights, the diversification of property rights, and the separation of state ownership from the enterprise's property rights. The roles of the exclusive state-owned company and the limited liability company are limited in the reform of state-owned enterprises because their assets are not divided into stocks, property rights cannot be transferred easily, the administrative structure of the corporation is not very strict, with no supervision from the public.

The limited stock companies have a high degree of openness. The state of business operation of an enterprise can be reflected by the fluctuations of its stock price. The achievements of the enterprise managers can also be judged by this, thus providing an objective and convenient method of appraising and improving the results of operations. Therefore, the introduction of the stock system will be a powerful impetus to changing the business operation mechanism of state-owned enterprises.

One, raising social financing as widely as possible through the adoption of the stock system to solve the problem of acute shortages of funds, the difficulties in renewing the existing equipment and enterprises debt, while at the same time shifting social consumption funds to investment funds. Two, giving the introduction of the stock system a wider scope. Experiments should be permitted in all fields where the stock system can be adopted, and especially in infrastructure facilities and basic industries and public utilities where the stock system can be taken to solve bottleneck problems. All large, medium-sized and small state-owned enterprises can benefit from the introduction of the stock system. Three, abolishing the state monopoly on the ownership of stock in the general fields of competition and permit non-state-owned enterprises to make investments and hold the controlling stock in order to adjust the structure of state-owned assets. It is especially necessary to have a correct understanding of the problems arising from stock controlled by overseas capital. If they are not permitted to hold the controlling stock, they have no incentive to investment. We should emancipate our minds even more on the question of overseas capital controlling stock in state-owned enterprises not vital to the national economy and the livelihood of the people, and set no limits on it.

China should abolish the "double-track stock system" and circulate the state-owned property rights to ensure the preserved

CHAPTER IV TRANSFORMATION UNDER A CORPORATE SYSTEM

value and increment of state-owned assets in the course of introducing the stock system.

In the "double-track system" of the Chinese stock market at present, state-owned stocks and individual stocks do not have the same rights or the same interests, thus seriously hindering the healthy development of the Chinese stock market and the preserving of the value of the state-owned stock. If the existence of the double-track system in the stock market made sense in its initial stage, it now has become an irrational problem in the development of the stock market. Therefore it must be changed to a single track system. The stock of a newly approved company, as long as they are common stock with no regard to ownership, should be listed for sale according to law after they are permitted to go public. All holders of this common stocks, whether Chinese or overseas, public or private, should enjoy equal rights on the basis of the percentage of stocks they hold.

The problems of irregularity have cropped up in the current stock system during the course of these experiments. Their main manifestations are: The evaluation of assets is not standard, there are no unified standards for defining property rights, the status of the representative of the property rights of the state-owned assets is confusing, the rights and interests of the stock holders are not equal, and enterprise management is unsuited to run the stock companies. The stock system has to be standardized in practice, but because the application of the stock system in the reform of state-owned enterprises in China is an experiment, there is no ready example to follow. Moreover, the stock system is still in the experimental stage. When there is no definite understanding and practical experience on many questions, it is impossible to adopt standards in one step. Therefore, a lengthy process is required to standardize the stock system, and only through the development of this system can it be standardized.

(II) To ensure the standardization of reforms in the corporate system, it is first necessary to make clear the motives for reorganizing state-owned enterprises into companies.

What is this motive? A correct answer to this question is

relevant to the solution of difficult problems in reorganizing state-owned enterprises into companies.

One, changing the operation mechanism. Namely, changing the enterprises' business operation mechanism by reorganizing them into companies to separate the functions of the government from those of the enterprise to enable the enterprises to conduct independent business operations, assume the responsibility for profit and loss, and achieve development and self-restraint. According to a survey conducted by Chinese entrepreneurs between December 1993 and May 1994, the main reasons cited for reorganizing state-owned enterprises into companies was to change the business operation mechanism of the enterprises.

Two, raising funds. It means to reorganize state-owned enterprises into companies and open new channels for obtaining short-term loans for construction to solve the difficulty of maintaining expanded production simply by depending on state investment. Therefore, people need Karl Marx's famous saying on the company that if one had to wait for accumulation to enable single capital to grow to the degree of being able to build railways, Marx was afraid that there would have been no railway in the world even by today. However, the job as done in an instant by concentration through the stock company. Moreover, in choosing a form for these new companies people have put the stock company at the top and are eager to organize them into listed companies.

Three, defining property rights and harmonizing the relations of these rights. The stock system is a good form for making clear the property rights of an enterprise, separating ownership from the right of business operations, and freeing the enterprises totally from the administrative control of the government.

Four, arousing the enthusiasm of staff and workers and increase the enterprise's cohesive force. By issuing stock to its employees, employees' interests are more closely linked with the company's interests, thus enhancing the company's cohesive force.

Five, modernizing enterprise management. In the course of developing and perfecting the system, the company should estab-

CHAPTER IV TRANSFORMATION UNDER A CORPORATE SYSTEM

lish a set of scientific management mechanisms so that all activities can be carried out efficiently. This management mechanism should not only suit the requirements of modern socialized commodity production, but more importantly must raise the operational efficiency of the company's assets. This is of practical significance to enterprise reform in China.

All the reasons for reorganizing enterprises into companies stated above are rational so far as the functions of the companies are concerned, but they are not sufficient. These motives fail to grasp the essence of organizing state-owned enterprises into companies. That essence is to remold enterprises into true main bodies of market operations. And this should become the fundamental motive.

The purpose of reorganization is to solve the problem fundamentally so that enterprises will be corporations in both name and actuality. First, in accordance with Article 4 of the Company Law, "the company enjoys all corporate property rights formed by the investments of the stockholders." And "the stockholders of the company as the investors enjoy the right in sharing the profit from the owners' assets, in making important decisions and choosing the managers on the basis of the amount of investment made in the company by the investors." The properties of the company and the properties of the stockholders are separated. Second, in accordance with Article 3 of the Company Law, the company is liable for its debts with all its assets, while the stockholders are liable to the company only with their own stock. In this way, the company undertakes independent business operations and assumes sole responsibility for profit and losses according to law with all its properties. Only in this way can the company enter the market as a truly independent entity. It can thus be seen that in the course of organizing state-owned enterprises into companies, the goal of remolding the participant in market operations is paramount. Only when an enterprise has corporate status can it effectively change its operation mechanism, raise and use funds reasonably, and exercise scientific management with both division of labor and restrictions.

(III) The operation of state-owned stock should be standardized.

1. Principles for the standardized operation of state-owned stocks.

In the course of reorganizing state-owned enterprises into companies, stocks are divided into state-owned stocks, corporate stocks and stocks held by employees. This is a realistic reflection of social and economic life. As long as no differences are artificially created among them, such divisions should not give rise to any evil. The main point is that the operation of state-owned stock should be standardized. The principles and criteria for this are:

First, the principle of equal rights among all stocks should be adhered to. (1) According to the provisions of the Company Law, the contents and scope of the rights enjoyed by all stockholders should be identical. The rights enjoyed by corporate stock should also be enjoyed by state-owned stock, and the rights which corporate stock does not enjoy should also not be enjoyed by state-owned stock. (2) Like other stock, the criteria for state-owned stock to exercise rights are the stocks themselves, namely, equal rights for each share, not equal rights for each shareholder. (3) The opportunities to exercise these rights are the same, namely, all stocks have equal opportunity to exercise common interest rights, but have no other right to intervene with the company. They all have the opportunity to exercise self-interest rights, including the distribution of interest and the distribution of properties when the company is disbanded, but have no other opportunity to benefit from the company. Like other stockholders, the holders of state-owned stock have the opportunity to gain through market sales. Correspondingly, they also have the same obligation to take risks.

Second, this is conducive to the operation of the company according to law. The operation of the modern limited stock company depends on the reasonable division of labor, mutual restraint, and the activities of management. Among these activities, the meeting of the stockholders as the receptacle of power is responsible only for decisions on matters under discussion limited

CHAPTER IV TRANSFORMATION UNDER A CORPORATE SYSTEM

to its function. It has neither the right nor the obligation to handle the company's day-to-day operations. The board of directors is responsible for decisions on company operations and business, but it must appoint managers to run the business. The chairman of the board of directors represents the company and the board of supervisors exercises supervision over the board of directors and the managers according to law. These organizational and rights structures as defined by the Company Law are relatively stable, and the key point is that the stockholders must exercise their rights through the stockholders meeting, but shall not intervene in the day-to-day operations in the name of individual stockholders.

Third, holders of the company stocks are shareholders. The acquisition of stock can be either original or inherited. In the first case, stockholders purchase the stocks; and in the second, the stock is acquired through transfer or by inheritance. In both cases they become stockholders in the company without exception and exercise their rights as stockholders. These principles apply to all stocks of the company, including corporate and state-owned stocks.

2. Confirmation of the state-owned stock.

In the course of reorganizing state-owned enterprises into companies, the confirmation of the shareholders of the state-owned stocks is a question that cannot be evaded. Of the existing state-owned enterprises, some were built with investment from the central government, and some with investment by the local governments. In the latter case, the investments were made by the governments of the provinces (municipalities directly under the central government and autonomous regions), counties (cities) and townships (towns). Therefore, when state-owned enterprises are reorganized into companies, the state-owned stock is held at multiple levels because investment comes from different sources. This reflects the situation of the properties of state-owned enterprises. If this reality was not recognized, and all properties formed by investments from any level of government were called state-owned stocks, many companies could not have been established.

If the shareholders of state-owned stock is confirmed as above, it is very possible to have holders of state-owned stock at several levels in one company. Are the relations among them relations of subordination or relations among equals? It is, of course, a relationship among equals according to the principles described above. Because the principle of lower levels subordinate to the upper levels applies only to the relations of administrative subordination, such relations do not exist among state-owned stockshoulders of different levels. The principle of one stock, one right applies to different stockholders of the same company, whether they are holders of the central state-owned stock or holders of local state-owned stock.

3. Who should be authorized to hold state-owned stock.

There is the question of who should be authorized to hold state-owned stock at whatever level of government. Proposals differ on this question:

One, the Administration of State Property shall be authorized to hold the state-owned stock. To the extent that there are different levels of state-owned stocks, the administrations of state property at the different levels shall be authorized to hold this stock.

Two, the original administrative department in charge of the enterprises shall be authorized to hold state-owned stock.

Three, the financial departments of the state shall be authorized to hold state-owned stock.

Four, the state assets investment corporations or state-owned assets management corporations shall be authorized to hold state-owned stock.

Five, enterprises shall be authorized to hold state-owned stock.

Six, an administrative commission for state property under the legal supervision of the people's congresses and their standing committees at all levels shall be set up as the representatives of the state property.

According to an investigation report on the share-holding enterprises made by the Chinese Entrepreneurs' Investigation System, the choices of existing entrepreneurs from among the

CHAPTER IV TRANSFORMATION UNDER A CORPORATE SYSTEM

above proposals were the following: First, whether judging by the overall situation or by the listed companies, unlisted companies, new companies or reorganized companies, less than 20 percent of those surveyed agreed to have the original administrative departments in charge of enterprises and financial departments of the state hold the state-owned stock. Second, only 27 percent of entrepreneurs agreed to be entrusted by the state to hold state-owned stocks. Third, nearly same percentages of entrepreneurs, 30.3 percent and 31.9 percent respectively, agreed to have the administrations of state property and state property investment corporations hold state-owned stocks. Of them, 43.5 percent of the listed companies are for the corporations and 33.1 percent of the unlisted companies are for the administrations of state properties.

This investigation tells us that the proposal for authorizing the original administrative departments and financial departments to hold state-owned stock has been abandoned in practice, and there is no need for further discussion. The four other proposals should be judged by the convenience of exercising the right to hold these stocks and the characteristics of the structure of the organization of the current Chinese system.

(1) There is no doubt that the Administration of State Property is an administrative organ for state property, but the administration of state property and the management of state property are two different questions. The former belongs to the category of the government exercising the right of economic administration, while the latter belongs to the category of exercising ownership. Considering that the two functions of administrative power and ownership of the state should be exercised separately, it is not appropriate to blend them into one. Therefore, the Administration of State Property should not be the holder of state-owned stock.

(2) It is also inappropriate to authorize the limited stock companies to hold their own state-owned stock. The Chinese Company Law not only negated the idea of the so-called "enterprise stocks," but also made strict provisions on the ownership of its own stock by companies. Article 149 of the law states: "A company shall not purchase its own stocks, except to write off

stocks in order to reduce its capital or to merge with other companies which hold its stocks." It also provides that "after purchasing its own stocks in accordance with the previous section, the company shall write off these stocks in 10 days and register for the change and make an announcement on it in accordance with the laws and administrative regulations." Although authorizing a company to hold state-owned stock and purchasing the company's stock are not exactly the same, they are undoubtedly very similar. This not only makes it easy to create false ownership of stock, it also makes it easier for the company to manipulate the stock market because of its inside information, thus infringing on the legitimate rights and interests of other stockholders. Therefore, it is not appropriate to authorize a company to hold its state-owned stock.

(3) The motive for setting up administrative committees for state property under the people's congresses and their standing committees at all levels is an attempt to separate the function of exercising the ownership of state property from the administrative organs. However, the people's congresses and their standing committees at all levels are organs of state power, whose supreme duty is to exercise supervision over administrative, judicial and military organs. If administrative committees for state property are set up in the people's congresses and their standing committees at all levels, the organs of state power will become administrative, making it very difficult to exercise supervision over their property rights, including the ownership of stock. Moreover, as they become administrative, they also have difficulty in exercising supervision over other organs. Therefore, a practice violating the system of the Chinese state organs is undesirable.

(4) It will be more feasible for the state to separate the right of administration of state property from the right of management, and authorize the Administration of State Property and state investment companies or state property management companies to exercise these respective rights. This will not only meet the state requirements to exercise the right of administration and the right of ownership separately, but also make it easier to harmonize relations on all sides. When the state investment companies or

CHAPTER IV TRANSFORMATION UNDER A CORPORATE SYSTEM

state property management companies are authorized to hold the state-owned stock, they themselves should also be standardized. First, these companies should be companies with exclusive state capital, set up and put into operation strictly in accordance with the Company Law. They should not become administrative companies or para-administrative companies, and they should have no administrative functions. Second, it should exercise the rights of the stock strictly in accordance with the provisions of the Company Law, including the observance of all its articles, both the substantive articles and the procedural articles. When necessary, special laws should be formulated to govern the exercising of the rights of the stockholders by these companies, but they should not contradict the provisions of the Company Law. Furthermore, these companies should not be restricted by the division of the industries, but rather be permitted to make investments and hold stock in all industries, trades and enterprises. Lastly, they must focus their attention on the management and operation of the state property, including decisions on selling state-owned stock and purchasing other stock. It is inappropriate to freeze state-owned stock, even less so to become the "keepers" of state property.

4. State-owned stock should be put into market circulation.

There is no doubt that all stocks have three functions. One, the function of control, namely, control of the companies by controlling and holding their stock; two, the function of profit, namely, receiving dividends and shares of the remaining property when the companies are disbanded; three, the function of speculation, namely, the receipt of extra-company profit through speculative activities in the stock market. These three functions are interrelated, not completely isolated from each other. It is true that the functions of control and profit are the most basic functions, but they are exercised through the speculative activities of the stock market. The function of speculation can not be exercised independent of the functions of control and profit, and is often manifested in these functions. The effective fulfillment of these functions depends on the company's operation according to law and a legitimate stock market. Otherwise, it is very difficult for these functions to play their roles. Because state-owned stock is not circulated in the market, and its functions are deformed. That is, it has only the functions of control and profit, but not that of speculation. It is exactly for this reason that the functions of control and profit alone cannot produce satisfactory results. This is manifested in the fact that the chance to increase value through the stock market is lost. In light of this, the stock market should be open so that state-owned stock can circulate like other stocks. Of course, the state-owned stock holds a controlling position in many of the limited stock companies. Under such circumstances, the unlimited entry of these stocks into the stock market might lead to an imbalance in the structure of the market and even to stock manipulation, thus infringing on the legitimate rights and interests of small investors. However, these limits should not come from the Company Law. The holders of state-owned stock can retain the right to transfer them or give up that right. But out of the need to maintain openness and equitability in the stock market and protect the public interests of society, the stock laws and other relevant laws and regulations should set the limits. However, such limits should apply not only to state-owned stock, but to all stocks.

5. The chairman of the board and general manager and their relations with the department in charge of the original enterprise.

According to the investigation report on the stock companies cited above, 60 percent of the chairmen of the boards and general managers of the existing companies received their posts through legal procedures. That is, the chairmen were elected by the boards of directors and the general managers were appointed by the boards of directors. However, improper intervention from the original administrative departments in charge is still widespread. The chairmen and general managers in more than 30 percent of the companies were not actually retained in the standard way. They were first elected and appointed and then approved by the departments in charge, or first chosen by the departments in charge and then elected and appointed by the boards of directors, or appointed directly by higher levels and then endorsed by the boards of directors. The companies reorganized from the old

CHAPTER IV TRANSFORMATION UNDER A CORPORATE SYSTEM

state-owned enterprises suffer most from the intervention of administrative departments at the higher levels, and more than 40 percent of these companies are still controlled by these departments. No doubt this state of affairs is the outcome of the traces of the old economic system. To change this, it should be stressed that the limited stock companies must follow the principle of "separating enterprise ownership from enterprise management." It means the partnership conference represents owners and the board of directors, managers. Obviously, selection of the chairman and general manager is a matter for the management level, and it's undesirable for the owners to intervene. Whether the original department in charge first chooses the chairman of the board and general manager or approves the elected chairman and general manager, it means that the owners are intervening directly with the management of the company, thus blurring the lines of demarcation between owners and managers. This is incompatible with procedures of the modern limited stock company. The Chinese Company Law fully reflects the mechanism for the company's multi-level operation, with the right of investors to discuss matters and make decisions limited only to the partnership conference. In order to give full play to the role of the board of directors, especially in electing the chairman and appointing the general manager, it is essential to implement the relevant provisions of the Company Law so that the board of directors is truly held responsible for selecting the chairman and general manager, and the interests of management are fully protected.

(IV) Regulations governing stock held by staff and workers should be standardized.

Stock held by staff and workers refers to the company stock held by its staff and workers.

The stocks held by staff and workers should be regarded as the company stocks held by individuals in society. So the stock of the staff and workers should have the same rights and obligations as the stocks held by individuals in society. The difference between them is that the company set aside a certain percentage (the percentage should be provided in the laws and regulations) of stock for the staff and workers to subscribe to with priority when it was established, and it also sets aside a certain percentage for the staff and workers when it issues new stock. Based on the above analysis, the circulation of the individual stock held by the staff and workers should not be restricted. After the individual stocks are standardized, they should be permitted to go public. Considering that the individual stocks held by the staff and workers were purchased at a lower price than those purchased by individuals in society it shall be stipulated that these stocks can be transferred after a given period of time, but it is improper to ban the transfer. Moreover, in order to facilitate the control over individual stock held by staff and workers, it might be a good idea to set up an "association of individual stockholders," but participation should be voluntary. Moreover, unless entrusted by holders of the individual stock, the association has no right to exercise the rights of stockholders on their behalf.

Chapter V
Reorganization of State-Owned Enterprises and Their Liabilities

I. The Significance and Methods of Reorganizing State-Owned Enterprises

(I) **With a view to invigorating the state-owned economic sector as a whole, we should advance the reorganization of state-owned enterprises to achieve the optimum combination of production and the allocation of resources.**

Reform of state-owned enterprises is not aimed only at bringing these enterprises back to life, but at invigorating the entire state-owned economic sector. It will bring "an end to a small number of enterprises and keep the majority alive." It will emphasize large and medium-sized state-owned enterprises, innovate the enterprise system, and reconstitute enterprises' organizational structure. This will promote the circulation and reorganization of assets in order to adjust and optimize the product mix, the industrial structure, and the enterprise structure. This will insure that products are marketable, efficiency is improved, and the costs are lowered, thus strengthening the quality and vigor of the entire national economy.

The reorganization of enterprises refers to the modification of their organizational form through changes in the principles of property rights. More concretely, it aims to reestablish the enterprises through alliances, mergers, annexation, sales, bankruptcies, and contracting and leasing. It includes changes in property organization and the structure of debts receivable and payable. For example, after reorganization, a more powerful company or group company, or a company with more specialized production is established, its organization is improved, capital funds increased, and its liabilities and cost of production lowered. As a result, the enterprise improves its adaptability to the market and its competitiveness so much that it can stand firmly and continue to grow stronger in the constantly changing marketplace of competition.

Further analysis shows that reorganization of enterprises is merely a means to an end. Its ultimate goal is the optimum combination and allocation of assets. The enterprise in the market economy is the means to achieve the best combination of production elements to form superior productive forces. Its role is to form an optimum combination of all production elements including materials, culture, technologies and capital for the most efficient production and business operations necessary to achieve the greatest results. The elements of the modern market economy, such as material and technological conditions, change constantly, making the old methods of production outdated and inefficient. Fierce competition means that enterprises must make constant adjustments of their component parts to assure efficient recombinations. The reorganization of an enterprise is an effective way of recombining its various elements. Essentially, reorganization of an enterprise is the means, recombination of the elements is the end, and the optimum allocation of resources is the final objective. Reorganization helps release the productive forces of the original enterprise. For example, the consequences of the annexation, joining and separation of enterprises must be the readjustment of production, the concentration of the means of production, and large-scale production or specialized production and elimination of overstaffing. In short, by relying on such adjustment to recombine and reallocate production elements, including the movement of the labor force, enterprises can become more effective and efficient.

The significance of reorganization of enterprises and the circulation and combination of assets in China at present can be summed up by the following points:

1. Exploring the idle productive capacity of the economy.

A major defect in the traditional planned economic system

CHAPTER V REORGANIZATION OF STATE-OWNED ENTERPRISES

is the lack of a facility for self-adjustment. As the enterprises are the subsidiaries of the government administration, their task is merely to organize production according to the mandatory plan of the government. This system fundamentally negates the enterprise's self-adjustment, thus preventing self-adjustment of the whole economy. The contradictions and structural imbalances in this type of economic operation are eliminated only through actions by the government from above. Because it is impossible for traditional government adjustments to be made in a timely fashion, such adjustments are possible only when the accumulated imbalances and contradictions became acute and a major reordering of the economy is then necessary. Moreover, traditional governmental adjustments were not made by economic means, but by administrative orders, often causing friction and resistance. Friction in the adjustments meant that these adjustments were futile, and except for the closing down of factories, suspension of production, merging of enterprises, and shifting of production from one product to another by mandate, many imbalances remained unchanged throughout the economy. It can be seen that the enterprise's behaviors under the traditional planning system and the governmental way of planned adjustments have determined this economic rigidity and structural ossification, making change difficult. In the use of the assets, once the fixed assets are formed they become stock assets and are permanently positioned in the enterprises where they grow, become old and sick, and die. It is then difficult to recombine them among other enterprises. Therefore, the unreasonable combination and inefficient use of production capability, and slow and stagnant circulation not only remain, but become more serious. It is estimated that the idle portion of fixed assets comes close to one third of total capability. This clearly shows that economic waste is huge, and efficiency is very low. In order to establish the market system so that enterprises can make independent decisions, it is necessary to set up a mechanism for reorganizing assets. This needed both to establish the socialist market system and to invigorate the idle assets to fully utilize China's economic potential.

2. The enterprises complement each other with their respec-

tive advantages to promote development.

To invigorate state-owned enterprises it is necessary to combine innovations in the system with solving the historical problems and present difficulties. The most urgent task is to free enterprises from the historical burden of heavy debt, redundant employment, and the running of community affairs to enable them to compete with non-state enterprises on an equal basis. To this end, the government should provide them with the necessary support. When the state is short of funds, it is a desirable policy to increase the strength of the enterprises and promote their development at less cost and with better results.

3. Relying on reorganization to turn losses into profits.

At present, 40 percent of state enterprises operate at a loss and smaller state-owned enterprises are the biggest losers. Therefore, it is necessary to develop new marketable low-cost quality products. The development of new products requires technology, funding, and marketing channels. These problems should not be solved by each enterprise independently, but rather by complementing each other and taking advantage of their respective strengths. So far as technical innovation is concerned, each enterprise imports its own production line and this has become an important cause of the heavy debt and difficult circumstances experienced by many of them. According to an investigative report from Liaoning Province, 50 percent of the debt incurred there since 1990 is for imported technologies. However, if these technical innovations are not made, it is difficult for the enterprises to invigorate production; and if they are made, it is difficult for them to avoid incurring new debt. Both new and old debts are difficulties faced by most enterprises. In order to adjust the product mix and raise technical standards to upgrade the products, it is totally necessary to establish the mechanism for the re-combination of assets among the enterprises through reorganization of the enterprises. This will be conducive to putting an end to losses and increasing profits. It will also enable enterprises to make technical innovations and prevent the growth of new debt.

4. Strengthening key enterprises by recombining assets.

CHAPTER V REORGANIZATION OF STATE-OWNED ENTERPRISES

The reform of key state-owned enterprises must be stressed. Efforts must be made to invigorate a great many large and high-tech enterprises. Since reform began 15 years ago, a number of state-owned enterprises, especially the larger ones, have increased their effectiveness and demonstrated strong growth. Many of these enterprises have increased their annual output value to several billion yuan, and some are nearing the 10 billion yuan mark. However, the principal restricting factor remains capital. The 500 top state-owned enterprises, once this restriction is removed, will grow into key and pillar industries of the state sector of the economy. In a short period their combined value could amount to 50 percent of the entire state sector. By relying on these key enterprises we will be able to redevelop the state-owned economic sector. And the most effective method for removing capital restrictions is the reorganization of enterprises.

5. Optimizing integrated combinations to improve the quality of the state-owned economic sector.

The reform of state-owned enterprises in China has entered a new stage of combining reform with reorganization and transformation with the aim of invigorating and developing the entire state-owned economic sector. It is necessary to readjust and reorganize state-owned enterprises in all industries in accordance with the requirements of the fundamental system of socialism, in keeping with the needs of the international market economy, and in the light of the new situation after the restoration of China's membership in the World Trade Organization.

6. Promoting changes in the old system and establishing the new mechanisms.

The principal form for reorganizing enterprises is to form them into companies and establish the modern enterprise system. This reorganization is conducive to the integration, and grouping of enterprises and is also beneficial to their annexation and mergers. Moreover, the economic integration of enterprises and their marriage to rural enterprises and joint ventures will enable state-owned enterprises to introduce new mechanisms conducive to deepening reform.

Since the beginning of reform, the government has encouraged the integration of enterprises with a view to invigorating state-owned enterprises, perfecting the structure of their organization, and raising their economic productivity. The Bankruptcy Law was formulated in 1986 and encourages the bankruptcy, annexation, and reorganization of state-owned enterprises. More importantly, with the deepening of reform, as these enterprises have been given power and responsibilities, they have started various forms of reorganization.

1. Reorganization through bankruptcy, annexation, and purchase. Although this form has just begun, it is an important method for adjusting the organization of state-owned enterprises and optimizing the recombination and allocation of state-owned assets.

2. Reorganization through the integration of whole industries. Some enterprises producing the same product or related products and parts have integrated their operating assets and formed limited liability or limited stock companies. The reorganization of several enterprises and all their properties into one company is conducive to the development of stable scale operations and plays an important role in developing the large-scale production of such consumer goods as automobiles and motor bicycles.

3. Reorganization through integration of enterprises of different sizes with one enterprise at the center. A core enterprise producing one major product can integrate with other enterprises making related products or parts to form a closely knitted center and then link with other enterprises in peripheral ties of production and business operations to form a loosely knitted entity. This can be done through contracting, leasing, and the distribution of products and profit, thus forming a large trans-regional enterprise group embracing scientific research, industrial production, trade, and banking. Such integration of enterprises, which reorganizes a large number of related enterprises, is an effective way to reorganize assets.

4. Reorganization by partial integration of assets. In this scheme, the original enterprise remains unchanged, but it uses the profitable and competitive part of its assets, for example, a

CHAPTER V REORGANIZATION OF STATE-OWNED ENTERPRISES

workshop, to form a company directly under the general works or a subsidiary, and then integrates it with other state-owned enterprises, township enterprises or joint ventures. This method of reorganization not only invigorates the stock value of enterprise, but forms new production capacity through the combined assets of the enterprises.

5. Reorganization through joint ventures and cooperation. An enterprise takes advantage of its resources—technologies, funds, business credibility, and trademarks—to organize cooperative production, lease other enterprises, or form joint ventures, including Chinese-foreign joint ventures and cooperation.

6. Reorganization through separation. China may separate original enterprise into several independent legal entities, or turn them into an enterprise group of subsidiaries and small enterprises under a holding company.

The traditional enterprise in China is "all-inclusive factory" doing everything from processing raw materials to turning out finished products. They are not only large and all-inclusive, but also run "community affairs." In a market economy, these enterprises must be simplified and separated from their present services and public welfare functions. This is known as "separation" or "making it small." "Small" refers to the abolition of non-production units and social services. This does not mean a reduction in production or output value. Quite the contrary, it makes the enterprises more specialized and enables them to concentrate on their primary products while reducing costs. It can be seen that reorganization of enterprises does not mean only the integration and merging of factories, but must be combined with necessary and reasonable separation as well. So reorganization through separation is a necessary way of recombining assets for their optimum allocation.

(II) Reorganization of enterprises is essential for establishing the market economy.

Reorganization of enterprises and the recombination of assets is a mechanism of the market economy. It is a voluntary act of the enterprises as a participant in a market driven by interests.

REFORMING CHINA'S STATE-OWNED ENTERPRISES

Since the initiation of reform and opening to the outside world, China has greatly aroused the enthusiasm of its enterprises by giving them more decision-making power and profit and allowing them to adopt different forms of business operations, including contracting and leasing. Moreover, the government has encouraged and promoted the integration of enterprises from above. Now, the voluntary reorganization and recombination of assets have begun, helping invigorate assets and make better use of everything. The cities which have successfully reorganized have shown greater productive force and higher growth. Generally speaking, however, the voluntary reorganization of state-owned enterprises and the circulation and reorganization of assets are still in a state of confinement. To ameliorate this situation it is essential to deepen overall reform and push forward the changing patterns.

1. Accelerating the change from the old pattern to the new and establishing the mechanism for the reorganization of enterprises.

Under the traditional system, there is no mechanism for the voluntary reorganization of enterprises and the circulation and reorganization of assets. Planned reorganization by the government was, in fact, made only in the period of adjustment to the national economy. Moreover, closing down factories in large numbers has a negative effect. In order to set up a flexible and consistent mechanism with less negative effects, it is necessary to establish the socialist market system and introduce market regulation. At the same time, industrial policy must be strengthened to put the spontaneous adjustment of the enterprise organizations and the circulation and reorganization of assets under government control. Under the socialist market system, it is possible to establish this flexible, effective, healthy, and orderly mechanism for the readjustment of enterprises and reorganization of assets. The key is to deepen reform, bring innovations to the system, and establish the mechanism for the reorganization of enterprises.

2. Exercising the governmental function of macrocontrol and pushing forward the healthy reorganization of enterprises and the reasonable circulation and efficient reorganization of assets. The

CHAPTER V REORGANIZATION OF STATE-OWNED ENTERPRISES

self-adjustment of the market is spontaneous. It can help achieve healthy reorganization, but it can also take a destructive form. For example, when a large number of enterprises go bankrupt, throwing a great many people out of work, economic and social shock ensues. Under market influences, an aimless reorganization of enterprises will also lead to imbalances in products, trades and industries. So the spontaneous reorganization of enterprises may also include inefficient reorganization with negative effects. In order for reorganization to truly help further the optimum allocation of resources, it is essential to strengthen the state's guidance and control of the process. It should be particularly stressed that in China at present many conditions are not yet ripe and the economic mechanism for voluntary reorganization of enterprises is not yet fully formed. It remains difficult to begin reorganization of enterprises and assets, and the assets of inefficient operations can hardly be adjusted. On the other hand, the imperfections in the price system has led to blind reorganization in some enterprises with conspicuously low efficiency. As a result, the long line of unmarketable products grows longer, while the short line of marketable products shrinks. It can thus be seen that in order to reorganize enterprises and recombine assets, the government must effectively exercise the function of macro adjustment and control. The main duties and roles of the government are: (1) To formulate principles for the reorganization of state-owned enterprises and specific rules for guaranteeing the reasonable adjustment of enterprise organizations, and supervise the implementation of these principles and rules; (2) to make industrial policies and rules for the development of backbone industries and key trades, and use economic means to guide the adjustment of the structure of enterprise organizations and the circulation and reorganization of assets; (3) since China has a vast territory with varying conditions from region to region, governments at the provincial level should have the power to reorganize enterprises and assets; (4) to guide and control the reorganization of enterprises and fully arouse the enterprise's enthusiasm to form the mechanism for the reorganization of enterprises on their own.

II. The Necessity of Reorganizing the Liabilities of State-Owned Enterprises

(I) The heavy debt burden of state-owned enterprises has become a severe practical problem for the normal operations of the Chinese economy, especially for the development of the state-owned economic sector.

The severity of this problem is reflected in the unreasonable structure of assets and liabilities of state-owned enterprises. The assets of over 80 percent of these enterprises are basically supported by liabilities. Large numbers of enterprises operate with high debt rates, resulting in the heavy burden of interest and a deteriorating financial situation. This not only makes it difficult for these enterprises to continue normal production and business operations, but infringes on the rights and interests of the owners, thus becoming a practical obstacle to reform and innovation within the enterprise system. This problem is also reflected in the rise of the proportion of the bad creditor's right of state-owned specialized banks and the drop in assets. The debt owed to the creditors which are due but cannot be recovered far exceeded the banks' equity capital. The assets of the banks are in danger of being engulfed by huge amounts of debt, while state-owned banks face a serious credit crisis, restricting the process of transforming the specialized banks into commercial banks.

According to the Industrial and Commercial Bank, bad loans are classified in four categories: Bad debts, risks, misappropriations and overdue loans.

A great proportion of the bad loans are industrial loans, mostly concentrated in light industry, textiles, chemicals, metallurgy, and the petroleum and coal industries. Of the commercial loans, bad loans account for a large percentage in state-owned and collective commercial enterprises, mainly concentrated in wholesale commercial enterprises. Of the loans used for technical transformation, bad loans are found mostly in the machine-building, textile, and other light industries. An outstanding problem with loans issued by the industrial and commercial banks is

CHAPTER V REORGANIZATION OF STATE-OWNED ENTERPRISES

the growth of unpaid interest due, directly affecting the profit levels of the banks.

The economic results and changes in the economic mechanisms have become crucial to the next stage of reform. In reform of state-owned enterprises, the huge debt (mainly loans owed to state-owned specialized banks) is the most outstanding problem. If the debt problem is not solved, it will be difficult to take the other measures, such as changes in the property rights structure, the transformation of the stock system, the adjustment of stock assets, the change of product direction, mergers of enterprises, and the technical transformation of enterprises. From the point of view of state-owned specialized banks, the large number of bad loans possessed by state-owned enterprises have lessened the quality of bank assets. Neither the principal nor the interest of large numbers of loans can be paid in time, and the banks then must pour new loans into state-owned enterprises, thus harming the credit mechanism. This is also a big obstacle in the transformation of specialized banks into modern commercial banks. In this way the large numbers of enterprise loans have formed a knot between the reform of enterprises and that of the banks. It is a very urgent task at present to study the question of reorganizing the liabilities of state-owned enterprises to find a feasible way to untie this knot.

(II) In transforming themselves into companies, state-owned enterprises must solve the problems of inadequate investment and excessive loans.

Under the traditional planned economic system, the funds of state-owned enterprises mainly come from financial allocation. The investments for fixed assets rely totally on the appropriations in the financial plan, and a good part of the money, about 50 percent, comes from these financial allocation. Only the remainder comes from the banks. The banks have, in fact, played the role of "cashier" for the Ministry of Finance and the State Planning Commission. This state of affairs has changed dramatically since the start of economic reform, and the division of duties and responsibilities between state finance and the banks has been largely adjusted. The external source for enterprise funding has changed from mainly the finance department to mostly the banks. Since the Sixth Five-Year Plan period, many economists have pointed out that enterprises have relied more and more on indirect short-term loans from the banks. At the same time, a considerable number of enterprises have engaged in excessive borrowing from the banks, creating a difficult problem for the next stage of reform. These enterprises are now overburdened with debt and have no ability to undertake financial risks.

We have classified state-owned enterprises (and some enterprises with other ownership) into four categories:

In the first category are enterprises which have relied on excessive loans for expanded production with good results and the ability to pay their debts.

In the second category are those enterprises which have borrowed heavily for equity investment and have no ability to repay the principal of the loans at present. But generally speaking, they are in normal operation and basically able to pay the interest, and repay new, short-term loans. We call them as enterprises with inadequate investment but with satisfactory results. To the banks, the loans corresponding to the equity have the corresponding assets of the enterprises, and are different from bad debts.

In the third category are enterprises which have inadequate investment and suffer losses due to poor management. They have softened their financial restrictions, but do not have aggressive management. They not only have difficulty repaying their old debts, but continue to seek new loans from time to time. If these enterprises are not reorganized and cannot exercise the right of ownership, their situation will deteriorate and eventually lead to bankrupt.

In the fourth category are enterprises with inadequate investment and fewer assets than debts. Their corresponding bank loans can be cancelled after verification, except for the part that are made up for by the compensations from the cleared stocks. The corresponding item for cancellation in the liabilities column of the bank statement of assets and liabilities is the reserve fund for

CHAPTER V REORGANIZATION OF STATE-OWNED ENTERPRISES

bad debts or the capital stock. It should be explained that financially the enterprises without adequate assets to offset their debts are in fact different from the enterprises which must go bankruptcy. Part of the enterprises can still be possibly reborn after reconsolidation in the procedure of bankruptcy. This is why importance is attached to the reconsolidation by a good part of the bankruptcy law of the market economy and the relevant procedures.

A clear knowledge of the conditions within these four categories is very important for the future of enterprises reform. We can see that reform will be difficult for enterprises in the second and third categories. Their reform is closely related to reform of the banking system. For example, the ratio between equity funds and the funds borrowed by enterprises is now very imbalanced, and most typical of this are commercial and trade enterprises. The equity capital of a good portion of foreign trade enterprises amounts to only around 2 percent of their working capital, the remainder consisting of bank loans. Some industrial enterprises are still allowed to pay wages and carry on production while their products are overstocked, causing an overexpansion of bank loans and the extension of triangular debt. The financial restrictions on these enterprises are very soft. Under these circumstances, some enterprises seem to think that since they have overborrowed, it will make no difference if they borrow even more, and that the government will solve their problem in the end. In light of this situation the banks should have taken measures to restrict some enterprises from continuing to borrow. In the early 1980s, there was a stipulation that the circulating capital of an enterprise should account for 30 percent of its total, but in fact this guideline was never implemented. As revenues continue to shrink, it becomes impossible to put more investment into state-owned enterprises. The banks, which cannot handle this percentage, have relayed the criteria for issuing loans. Moreover, as the specialized banks have a more social agenda and must issue loans based on policy, they find it inappropriate to settle outstanding bad debts.

For aforementioned reasons a considerable number of state-owned enterprises have very low percentages of equity funds and are operating with excessive liabilities and great risks. Moreover, with these large debts, the enterprises have no incentive to assume responsibility for their profit and loss and little business enthusiasm. Especially for enterprises with an excess of liabilities over assets and with poor business operations, soft financial restrictions are even more obvious as applied to the question of loans. If an enterprise wants to change to a new administrative structure with incorporation as its starting point, it must first solve the problems of inadequate funds and large debt before it can be reorganized into a company.

The operation of an enterprise with huge liabilities, and the slow turnover of bank credit with poor quality assets are, in essence, the same problem reflected in two different industrial areas. Although the banks have been compelled to relax their terms for issuing loans by objective conditions such as multiple targets for bank operations, the need for policy loans, and pressure from the local governments, the objective consequences are that the bank risks have increased and it has become more difficult for the banks to strengthen their restriction mechanisms and operational disciplines.

(III) Determining the scope of the reorganization of enterprise liabilities in the light of their specific conditions.

1. Analyzing the enterprise's business activities and liabilities.

(1) Does the enterprise have a successful business operation with loans they can repay?

(2) Does the enterprise show a moderate profit, but with too many outstanding debts?

(3) Does the enterprise have fewer assets than liabilities and on the brink of bankruptcy?

2. Determining the scope for the reorganization of liabilities.

(1) The enterprises in the first category shall not have their liabilities reorganized because they are normal.

(2) The enterprises in the third category shall have their liabilities cancelled, as they are not included in the scope of reorganization. A part of their liabilities shall be offset by a part

CHAPTER V REORGANIZATION OF STATE-OWNED ENTERPRISES

of their assets, and the remainder shall be cancelled by using the bank reserve funds for bad debts. When the bank funds for bad debts are insufficient to cancel all liabilities, the amount of capital equivalent to the uncancelled amount of liabilities should be voided. This might cause an insufficiency of bank capital and should therefore be replenished by issuing stock. In this way the reorganization of the enterprises can be combined with the reorganization of the banks.

(3) Of the loans which the enterprises in the second and third categories have no ability to repay, the fixed asset loans and the flowing capital loans amounting to 30 percent of the fixed amount of flowing capital shall be taken as the objects for reorganization of liabilities; and the rights of the creditors shall be turned into the right to obtain stock. In this way the liabilities of the enterprises in the second category can be wholly turned into stock rights, and the liabilities of the enterprises in the third category can be greatly reduced.

(IV) The possibility of reorganizing liabilities between state-owned enterprises and banks.

The combination of bad debts in the state-owned economic sector and the oversupply of money arising from it have already led to inflation in China. In other words, the bad debts of state-owned enterprises have been digested by inflation, so the reorganization of liabilities in the state-owned economic sector will not in itself lead to new inflation.

No matter what the cause of inflation, it is ultimately reflected in an oversupply of money. Therefore, to control inflation it is essential to stop the increase of the money supply. The reorganization of liabilities should be made mainly through a change among the relations between the creditor's rights and the debts among the banks, enterprises, and financial departments. This process is not a factor affecting the money supply.

For the banks, the process of changing liabilities does not mean an increase in total credit. It only switches debtors from enterprises to financial departments. Moreover, the central bank's total assets do not increase, neither does the money supply.

Therefore, this will neither cause new inflationary pressure nor reduce current inflation. This being the case, what is the significance of changing the liabilities? The most significant goal is to strengthen financial restrictions to create conditions for the establishment of a modern enterprise system and equal participation in market competition for state-owned enterprises.

Under the current liability and enterprise system, the expansion of the state-owned economic sector and compensation for policy loan enterprise losses rely on bank loans, delayed payments among enterprises, and the use of the social security funds for employees. These are the hidden outstanding accounts of state finance. The continued increase of such accounts has caused inflation and disturbed the credit relations among the various sectors of society, making it difficult to establish normal credit order. If this situation is allowed to continue the consequence can only be an unchecked extension of inflation. Reorganization of liabilities will turn these hidden accounts into open accounts and allow the state to truly bear the burden of the liabilities. After the liabilities are reorganized, the financial function and the credit function can be strictly differentiated, hardening the budgetary restrictions of state-owned enterprises and gradually bringing inflation under control.

III. Methods and Measures for Reorganizing the Liabilities of State-Owned Enterprises

(I) Combing the shift of the bank's bad creditor's rights with the reform of the enterprise property rights system, and the reform of the state investment system.

How can the bad creditor's rights of the banks be shifted? One idea is to shift these rights of the banks while establishing a modern enterprise system and reforming the state investment system. The shift of the bad creditor's rights of the banks can be beneficial to the state, the banks, and the enterprises. For the state, it can shift the bad creditor's rights and the excessive

CHAPTER V REORGANIZATION OF STATE-OWNED ENTERPRISES

liabilities of the enterprises, thus encouraging state-owned enterprises and banks to change their systems. The banks can greatly reduce the losses from these loans, diversify ownership of assets, take part in management in the capacity of stockholder, and exercise direct supervision and control over credit assets to accelerate the change to commercial banks. For the enterprises, it reduces the pressure of paying the principal and interest of the bank loans, helps them improve management, and promotes change in the management mechanism. The creditor's rights of the banks can be shifted in the following five ways:

1. Changing the loans to investments or changing the creditor's rights to stock rights. The enterprises which cannot repay the bank loans, but which still have prospects for preserving and increasing the value of their assets, can change this debt into the bank's investments. The bank can then take part in management of the enterprise and protect the uncovered loans through their participation. For the enterprises which can be merged or integrated into joint ventures, the banks can change the current stock loans of these enterprises into indirect investments. Those enterprises which have development potential and the ability to adopt the stock system but at present have difficulty in repaying loans can change the bank loans into investments in the enterprises by having the banks buy their stock in the hope of diversifying risk and recovering the loans through future stock sales. On the other hand, the banks, after changing from creditor to stockholder, can take part in the supervision and control of the enterprises to ensure the safety and profitability of their investments. It should be pointed out that only part of the loans can be changed into stock, and the creditor's rights should not be changed into stock in enterprises facing possible bankruptcy to prevent bad loans from becoming bad investments.

2. Changing the loans into debentures. For enterprises with overdue loans but still with potential, the banks can change part of the loans into transferable debentures and recover the overdue loans by issuing enterprise debentures. The enterprises should not issue enterprise debentures for irrecoverable loans, nor change part of the loans into financial debentures and pour funds into

other enterprises with debts in order to repay the bank loans. However, the issuance of enterprise debentures is limited by the attractiveness of the issuing enterprises and the issuance of financial debentures is restricted by the ability of the economy to absorb inflation.

3. Auctioning the bank's creditors rights. China has adopted a number of preferential policies for enterprises with exclusive overseas investment and joint ventures, and overseas investors are generally interested in purchasing domestic enterprises. It can be considered that the banks can auction the irrecoverable rights of the creditor to the social investors, overseas businessmen, or intermediate investment organizations at discounts. The investors or intermediate investment organizations may turn the losses into profit by transforming the purchased enterprise and reaping profits from their investment when the enterprise goes public.

4. Auctioning the enterprise's property rights. For enterprises with fewer assets than liabilities or enterprises on the brink of bankruptcy, their property rights may be auctioned openly by creditors committees with participation of the banks. The income from the auction can then be used to repay the bank loans.

5. Issuing purchasing company debentures. China should set up purchasing companies with the banks participating or holding controlling interest to issue debentures, and use the income from the sale of the debentures to repay the bank loans. After the enterprises are transformed into new enterprises, the banks may sell the property rights of the new enterprises and use this income to make up for the bad loans and obtain profit from their investments.

Principles for the conversion procedure are as follows:

1. By changing the loans into investments or changing the rights of the creditor into the rights of stockholders, only a part of the bank loans can be changed into investments in the enterprises. This is the common practice of international banking institutions. As far as the enterprises are concerned, the targets for this conversion should be mainly large and medium-sized state-owned enterprises and enterprises with prospects for becoming stock companies in basic industries which are not allowed to

CHAPTER V REORGANIZATION OF STATE-OWNED ENTERPRISES

go bankrupt by the state. The scope of loans should be mainly those irrecoverable loans which the state should have allocated, but has not, and which have been carried by the banks for a long time. Moreover, in transferring the rights of the creditor, the banks and enterprises must take the risks into consideration and avoid changing bad loans into bad investments. Therefore the banks must prudently choose those enterprises suitable for the transfer of bad loans.

2. Changing loans into investments or the rights of the creditor into the rights of the stockholders should be done together with the reform of the state investment system, the reform of the property rights system, the transformation of the enterprises into stock companies, the reform of the state financial and tax system, and the changing of the state specialized banks into commercial banks. Otherwise it will be impossible to succeed in converting the creditor's right. The banks and enterprises should be permitted to experiment in a positive way to formulate plans and regulations that ensure standard and scientific reforms.

3. Changing loans into investments or changing creditor's rights into stock rights is one way to invigorate state-owned enterprises, but not the only way. We should try best to prevent from and avoid underestimating the value of state-owned assets, and leaving the enterprise's original debts and surplus staff and workers to the local government.

(II) Ideas for solving the problem of liability.

One way is to cancel the enterprise's liabilities after verification. That is to remove these loans from the bank's assets and at the same time cancel the corresponding part of reserves for bad debts from the bank's liabilities.

While it is true that cancelling enterprise debt is a great benefit to the enterprises, it is also a disadvantage for the banks. Because while cancelling creditor's rights from bank assets, a corresponding amount of capital is also cancelled from the bank's liabilities. This inevitably lowers the degree of sufficiency of the bank's capital, raises the prospects for risk-taking, and may even directly force some banks to fold. Moreover, the cancellation of enterprise debt inevitably encourages them to "take meals in the big canteen" of the banks. Therefore, this idea is undesirable.

The second solution is through state finance. There are two ways to go about this. One is for state finance to make allocations to enterprises so they can repay the bank loans and establish a standard debt-equity ratio. The other method is for state finance to make direct allocations to the banks to replenish their capital so they can cancel the enterprise's bad debts after verification.

The main problem with this idea is that because the total sum of this debt is very large, hundreds of billions of yuan (RMB), current state finance is unable to pay such a huge amount. If this is done anyhow, no matter how reluctantly, it can only cause a huge financial deficit, eventually leading to inflation. Moreover, this practice will accustom both the enterprises and the banks to "take more meals in the big canteen of the state."

The third idea is to make the debt-equity switch, changing the debt of enterprises into stockholder rights for the banks.

The practice of using the debt-equity switch to solve the problems of businesses with excessive debt has been adopted in some Latin-American countries. This practice is more reasonable than the first two methods since it embodies the principle of equal value in the market economy without increasing the financial burden. But there is also a question that should not be ignored. That is, after the switch from debt to equity, the banks' risk increases greatly by using bank deposits to buy stock causing the quality of assets to drop.

The fundamental problem ignored by these three ideas is that changes that should take place or have already taken place in the enterprise system, the banking system, and the financial system as well as the relations among them as the entire economy changes track, only considers the question of enterprise debt. In this way, it is hard to avoid paying attention to one aspect while losing sight of another. We should find a way to reform which can remove excessive debt burdens without increasing state expenditures, while guaranteeing the quality of bank assets.

On the one hand, through a debt-equity switch the debts can be turned into equity to relieve enterprises of their debt burden,

CHAPTER V REORGANIZATION OF STATE-OWNED ENTERPRISES

and on the other, by distributing stock warrants to the banks, the state permits the banks to buy enterprise stock to guarantee the quality of bank assets. This practice, for the time being, meets the needs of enterprises, banks, and the state finance. From a long-term point of view, the banks with which enterprises open accounts partly replace the state as owners, helping solve the fundamental question of the ownership of state-owned enterprises and marking the first step toward the establishment of a Chinese-style banking system. There still may be ideological obstacles in the current Chinese banking structure preventing the acceptance of omnipotent banks, but this can provide the framework for the separation of commercial banks from investment banks.

This idea may be gradually developed by the following steps:

Step one—the debt-equity switch between the enterprises and the banks.

After the switch from debts to equity, the banks themselves face some problems. Because the banks hold the rights to large quantities of enterprise stock entailing increased risk, the quality of the bank's assets may drop. At the same time, the cancellation of debt lowers bank capital. Also, the banks will become omnipotent banks when they both handle deposits and loans and make investments. This is different from the current idea of a central bank, and will make it more difficult to exercise macroeconomic control to a certain degree. But the omnipotent bank is the wave of the future in the world today, and there are profound reasons for this.

Step two—the solution to the problem of the division of business between commercial and investment banks is to make adjustment to the internal operations of the banks.

The specialized banks may be divided into two departments —a commercial department and an investment department. The investment banks can conduct direct investment business while the commercial banks can hold special types of securities (such as treasury bonds and investment bank debentures) as assets apart from deposits and loans. In this way, there will be internal division of labor, making it easier for the central bank to exercise supervision and control. Of course, the guiding principle here is to change the specialized banks into multi-functional banks with an internal business division. Unless this is accomplished it will be difficult to make the debt-equity switch.

After the banks adjust internally, there will still be problems with the commercial bank department. The quality of the assets of the commercial bank department depends on the evaluation of the securities of the investment banks, which they hold, and the risk evaluation of the securities issued by the investment banks depends on the financial situation of the enterprises in which they hold stock rights. Of these enterprises, some are already successful and some need to be transformed. In general, the quality of the assets of commercial banks is not high. In the investment bank departments there are also some problems, chiefly, capital is low and stock rights risks are rather high.

To solve these problems, it is necessary to take the third step.

Step three—the state gives the investment banks stock rights subscription warrants, and the banks use these warrants to buy successful enterprises.

In order to guarantee the quality of the investment banks, the state should inject new capital into the banks, not in the form of money, but in the form of these subscription warrants.

When this process is completed, the investment banks stock in successful enterprises through the use of the subscription warrants to raise the quality of their combined stock rights and the credibility of their securities. At the same time, when the quality of securities held by the commercial bank department rises, the quality of all assets will rise and the degree of risk fall. In this way, the problem of raising the quality of bank assets can be solved.

When this transformation is completed the investment banks can readjust the structure of their own assets appropriately, from the use of all assets for investment in enterprise stock rights to an exchange for assets with more fluidity to further improve their quality. Such a healthy structure will have further potential for profit from the revaluation of capital, including a rise in the market value of the enterprises and the investment and commercial banks themselves. These profits help replenish their own capital weakened by the cancellation of the bad debts. Of course, this does not exclude direct sales of stock rights of a small number of enterprises by the investment banks.

After the completion of this process, the problems of enterprise debt and the quality of the bank loans and sufficiency of bank capital will all be solved, and the relations between enterprises and banks will also undergo important changes to conform to the needs of the market economy. The banks will become part stockholders of enterprises and the structure of the enterprise's stock rights will also change. This structure will help form the long-term relations between the banks and the enterprises. International experience has shown that these long-term relations are of great importance to the development of productive forces. This will give rise to something the Japanese and German patterns of international competitiveness.

Such a structure will also have a powerful influence on the growth and development of the capital market.

(III) It is necessary to cultivate and develop intermediate organizations to participate in the reorganization of state-owned enterprises and solve their debt problem through the transfer of credit rights.

1. The necessity and feasibility of cultivating and developing intermediate organizations.

Introduction of intermediate organizations will play the role of using "one stone to kill two birds" in the "creditor's rights-stock rights" switch of the state economic sector. They can change the enterprise system while relieving state-owned enterprises of their bad debts, and change the original structure of sole state ownership of stock rights in state-owned enterprises through the intervention of the intermediate organizations to transform state-owned enterprises into limited liability companies or limited stock companies. This will eliminate the bad debts of the specialized banks and optimize the structure of their assets and liabilities, thus creating conditions for the change of specialized banks into commercial banks. The intermediate organizations can participate in the "creditor's rights-stock rights" switch through a large number of investment subjects, thus laying the foundation for the formation and perfection of the capital market in China. In this way, the intermediate organizations are similar to the converters for reform and innovation of the system. Their functions are to reorganize and transform the old system by absorbing idle funds and on this basis, to establish a new system and new operational mechanisms, thus giving the state economic sector new vitality so they will have the ability to enter into the market economy.

Judging from practical and existing objective conditions, it is not only necessary but also fully feasible to introduce to participate in the "creditor's rights-stock rights" switch in the state sector.

The intermediate organizations can provide a source of funds for the reorganization of liabilities and give enterprises a change for new development. So far as the current stock of social funds (as opposed to the financial funds) is concerned, the social intermediate organizations have adequate sources to provide funds corresponding to the amount of the bad debts of state-owned enterprises. First, with the rapid growth of the economy since the beginning of reform, many non-bank monetary institutions in China have acquired the capability to obtain short-term loans and participate in the supply of such funds. Second, the successful large enterprises or enterprise groups with investment and control ability now have the ability to expand their investments. Third, the savings and cash on hand of the Chinese people have been very impressive, and now exceed 2,000 billion RMB yuan. The absorption of the idle funds in some form can also help solve the problem of state-owned enterprise debt. Finally, there are abundant sources of overseas funds. As the economic growth rate in the developed countries is sometimes stagnant and international capital investment relatively low, the large consortiums, especially the investment companies with huge amounts of capital, seek developing countries and regions with relatively high returns or investment. China is undoubtedly now one of the hot countries they are interested in.

CHAPTER V REORGANIZATION OF STATE-OWNED ENTERPRISES

Preliminary market conditions are ripe for the intermediate organizations to participate in the "creditor's rights-stock rights" switch of the state economic sector. In the last three years, the development of the property rights business of state-owned enterprises has gained momentum, and all kinds of property rights business centers, exchanges, and corporations have mushroomed. And preliminary practical experience has shown that state-owned enterprises have now effectively promoted the allocation of resources, structural adjustment, the circulation of assets, and technical transformation. The preliminary formation of these tangible forms, as well as a large number of intangible forms of property rights, has provided adequate information and operational space for the participation of the intermediate organizations. The entry of the intermediate organizations into the property rights market and their becoming the subjects of the transactions help harmonize property rights relations and standardize the property rights transactions. This is of great importance to the development of the Chinese capital market.

2. The functions and types of intermediate organizations and the methods of their intervention.

(1) The functions of the intermediate organizations.

The basic duty of the intermediate organizations is to concentrate the funds of the investors at home and abroad in various forms and buy the creditor's rights of the specialized banks to hold the stock rights of state-owned enterprises which owe debts to these specialized banks. They also function to reorganize and reconsolidate enterprises to gradually increase their competitiveness in the market. On this basis, the intermediate organizations, depending on the rights and interests of the investors, get the interest and profit from the stocks and give reasonable returns to the ultimate investors.

To fulfill this purpose, the intermediate organizations should have consulting and operating ability.

That is, the ability to analyse and evaluate the business operations of state-owned enterprises, including information about the managers, industrial analysis, analysis of operations, investment projects, analysis of land and assets, and an evaluation of assets. The intermediate organizations should employ specialists who have authority and are knowledgeable on matters of legal evaluation of assets. They will also consult on liquidation and the change of the enterprise system. Chinese state-owned enterprises usually include both production and services in one complicated structure. They are involved in things like the operation of non-production service units (canteens, schools, hospitals and housing) which do not conform to the functions of economic entities and make it difficult for new investors to accept them. Therefore, in order to strip enterprises of these original non-productive services, the intermediate organizations should provide advice on the liquidation of assets, the working out of assets and liabilities, a detailed list of properties, and the formulation of liquidation methods.

The intermediate organizations should also have the ability to adjust the structure of the assets and liabilities of the enterprises by, on the one hand, reorganizing the assets in various ways, separating the operational from the non-operational assets, and transferring the non-operational assets to outside the enterprises, and on the other hand, by raising funds, buying part of the creditor's rights, reducing the enterprise debt, and expanding capital strength. Because what the intermediate organizations do in participating in the reorganization is to buy the bank's creditor's rights to hold stock rights in the enterprises, they assume great responsibility for the risks. It will take time before they are able to realize a profit. Therefore, the intermediate organizations should have the ability to seek opportunities for enterprises to go public. Going public will not only have an important impact on the involvement of intermediate organizations in the "creditor's rights-stock rights" switch, but also help accelerate the transformation of large and medium-sized state-owned enterprises into stock companies and promote the growth and maturity of the Chinese stock market.

Obviously, the existing financial institutions and asset management in China fall short of the duties and required abilities of the intermediate organizations described above. If they can be guided to take part in the reorganization of state-owned enterprises, it is possible to standardize behavior, improve the quality of their management, and create conditions for the growth and perfection of the capital market in China.

(2) The types and role of the intermediate organizations.

Depending on their nature and the scope of their business, the intermediate organizations are classified into two categories. In one category are the financial institutes, other than banks, dealing in trusts, insurance, and stock shares. In the other category are property sales organizations such as state-owned property sales companies, holding companies, and large enterprise groups companies.

a. Non-bank financial institutions.

By the end of March 1994, the non-bank financial institutions with Chinese capital set up lawfully with the approval of the People's Bank of China included: 391 trust and investment companies, 20 insurance companies, 14 short-term loan and leasing companies, and 91 stock companies. More than 220 foreign and overseas financial institutions have opened 330 offices in China, including three foreign insurance companies and four foreign investment financial companies.

Of these non-bank financial institutions, the various types will play different roles in the reorganization of state-owned enterprises and in the creditor's rights-stock rights switch.

The trust financial institutions. Their main source of income is the extra-budgetary funds of state-owned enterprises and organizations, a long-term term and highly stable source. Therefore, when they deal in trusts and investments they can invest their equity and trust funds in construction projects or enterprises. In the creditor's rights-stock rights switch, China may make use of the available business experience of the trust and investment companies to take part in the reorganization of those enterprises with prospects for development. Making investments in the form of stock rights in state-owned enterprises by purchasing the bank's creditor's rights in a selective way will help open business opportunities for the trust financial institutions.

Stock financial institutions. In recent years, the available securities such as government bonds, enterprise debentures and stocks, have diversified. Comparatively speaking, investment funds have broad advantages over other investment instruments because of their special form of "public investments under specialist management." Especially in the light of large savings deposits of both urban and rural Chinese, and because the broad masses of people have no knowledge of investment, the investment funds are an ideal instrument of investment for the general public. This, therefore, is a feasibility way to establish investment funds through financial institutions to attract large amounts of revenue from among the people and from overseas to accumulate long-term funds by which to take part in the creditor's rights-stock rights switch.

Insurance financial institutions. It is essential that these business operations use the insurance funds well and flexibly. On the one hand, the economic strength of the insurance companies shall be increased by raising insurance funds in various ways, and on the other, these funds shall be used reasonably to fulfil all insurance functions. The insurance funds are huge, stable resources for long-term use. Therefore, the insurance financial institutions can use the idle insurance premium income and reserve funds for investment to increase the value of these funds quickly.

b. The state-owned property sales organs.

As a result of the reform of state property management and operations, a number of state property management main bodies have merged in recent years. The principal forms include state-owned property sales companies, holding companies and large enterprise group companies. The formation of these property sales organs has opened new channels for the reorganization of state-owned enterprises.

Take the state-owned property sales companies as an example. The intermediate organizations for the management of state-owned assets, entrusted by the representatives of the owners of these assets, are entitled to the rights and interests of the investors in state-owned enterprises under their control, namely, making policy decisions on important investment projects, receiving profit from the increment of state-owned assets, and making decisions

CHAPTER V REORGANIZATION OF STATE-OWNED ENTERPRISES

on the disposal of state-owned assets by appointing representatives to ensure that the assets increase in value. The state-owned property sales companies usually evolve out of the original government departments in charge of enterprises, and therefore often have the trade and regional characteristics. In the course of the reorganization, the state-owned property sales companies can make use of their advantages to reorganize the assets and liabilities of state-owned enterprises within the limits of their authorization.

In the course of the reorganization, we can not only make use of the existing intermediate organizations and give them guidance and standardize them, but also create another group of new investment instruments, especially of the medium investment type, which can attract overseas funds to open Chinese and overseas joint ventures, and make use of their senior specialists and advanced managerial expertise to jointly participate in the reorganization of China's state-owned economic sector.

(3) The methods of involvement of the intermediate organizations and the problem of their interests.

In the course of reorganization, the intermediate organizations may become involved in several ways, either at the enterprise, trade, or industrial level.

China must face a great number of large and medium-sized state-owned enterprises which have lost their ability to repay their debts. Reorganization of these debts one by one at the enterprise level may be economical because it is entirely the act of the individual enterprises, but it will take time and effort, and the total cost will be great. Reorganization of enterprise debt at the trade or industrial level tends to be the act of the government. Maybe it will produce some results with smaller unit costs, but in the end this will depend on whether the government is really determined to begin with the thorough reorganization of state-owned enterprises. One thing is certain, that no matter how they become involved in the reorganization of state-owned enterprises, it will depend on choice through experience. Therefore, we will touch on the following methods of involvement on the basis of available experience and knowledge.

Involvement at the enterprise level. In the light of the experience of the past two or three years, ongoing reorganization of individual enterprises has adopted the form of equity financing of the financial institutions. Individual state-owned enterprises must do the following: First, they should make an inventory of the assets, evaluate them, liquidate the creditor's rights and debts, and check the state-owned capital stock; second, they should look into accounts according to standard practice, work out standard financial reports and supply them to those intermediate organizations which are interested in investing in the enterprise; third, the intermediate organizations, out of their own strategic consideration, they should work out a short-term loan plan and make the actual investment in enterprise; fourth, after the funds are available, they are used to repay the debts of the enterprise to adjust the structure of the assets and liabilities, invest in new projects to adjust the product mix, and attempt to solve the problem of making new arrangements for the redundant employees.

Involvement at the trade level. The typical practice is that of the state-owned property sales company. Because its predecessor was the administrative department in charge of the enterprises, the reorganization of assets and liabilities of enterprises at the trade level has more advantages. The general practice is: Bankrupt a number of small and medium-sized state-owned enterprises with fewer assets than liabilities which have long suffered losses, sell out a number of enterprises which have satisfactory economic results but do not conform to the industrial distribution system and have no long-term prospect for development, transform a number of good enterprises into limited stock companies, and concentrate some funds from profits to make additional injections of capital into a large number of enterprises with prospects for development.

Involvement at the industrial level. China presently has no practical experience in the reorganization of liabilities at the level of an entire industry. This is only an initial idea proposed on the basis of foreign experience and our research. Let us take a sub-branch office of a state-owned specialized bank in a certain

CHAPTER V REORGANIZATION OF STATE-OWNED ENTERPRISES

city as an example. First, an overall judgement of the bank's assets and liabilities should be formed and an analysis of the size and proportion of its bad debts, the cause for these bad debts, and the general enterprise conditions which led to the bad debts should be made. Second, under the overall coordination of the municipal government, the specialized bank and the intermediate organization jointly work out a plan for handling bad debt and select a number of trades and enterprises with prospects for development as targets for the switch from "the creditor's rights to the stock rights." Third, the intermediate organization buys the creditors' rights of the enterprise involved in the switch from the banks, and at the same time holds the stock rights of these enterprises. The combination investment from the investment funds will be a suitable form in this respect. Fourth, the state-owned bank optimizes the structure of assets, and state-owned enterprises turn part of their bad debts into capital stocks, and at the same time obtain a new opportunity because of the entry of these incremental funds.

In short, in whatever form intermediate organizations take part in the switch, intermediate organizations as enterprises will themselves always face the problem of profitability. Obviously, because what intermediate organizations buy in the reorganization are not highly profitable stocks, but rather the creditors' rights to bad debts, it is difficult for them to receive a large income in a short period of time. Moreover, the sources of funds of intermediate organizations mostly depend on the investment and trust business and the establishment of risk funds, large deposits and foreign exchange, and the investors of these funds want returns. Therefore, in order to guide and encourage intermediate organizations to take part in the reorganization and maintain the stability of their income, it is necessary to have a policy which broadens the scope of their business, and increases new sources of income.

Chapter VI
Reconfiguration of State-Owned Assets Management

I. The Present Situation and Problems of State-Owned Assets Management in China

The statistics of the State Administration of State-Owned Assets for in 1993 show that by the end of 1992 the state-owned assets in China totalled 3,069.7 billion yuan (RMB), including operating assets of 2,210.1 billion yuan and non-operating assets of 859.6 billion yuan. In the Chinese structure of industrial capital, state-owned industrial capital accounts for 73.1 percent. The total amount of state-owned assets is huge, and the state sector plays the leading role in the operation of the national economy. However, the management and operating mechanism of state-owned assets fails to suit the requirements for establishing the socialist market economic system. The relations of the property rights of state-owned enterprises are not harmonious, enterprises are shouldered with burdens, and the loss of state property is still very serious. According to reports from the provinces where state-owned assets were verified, the enterprises' net assets of the enterprises generally account for around 20 percent of the total assets. After verification of the assets was completed in the first group of more than 9,400 enterprises in 1993, about 40 percent of the enterprises were actually "propertyless enterprises." Statistics from the State Statistical Bureau shows that the proportion of state-owned industrial production to the total industrial output value dropped from 78.5 percent in 1979 to 44 percent in 1993, while the increment of the non-state industrial sector accounted

CHAPTER VI RECONFIGURATION OF STATE ASSETS MANAGEMENT

for 63.2 percent of the total increment of the industry in the past dozen years. The growth rate of the state sector of the economy is far behind that of the non-state sector.

The state-owned economic sector is playing the leading role in the socialist market economy, and is the chief source of state revenues. However, it should be seen that while total state-owned assets have increased, there are also some problems in the operation and management of these assets. These problems include poor economic results, the unreasonable structure of assets and asset loss.

—The economic results of state-owned enterprises remain unsatisfactory. The enterprises' inefficient operation and the problem of losses arising from it have always been a difficult problem that must be solved during the reform and development of the Chinese economy. In the past few years the enterprises' economic results have improved, but are still not what they should be. Inefficient operations have restricted the sustained and stable development of the national economy and imposed heavy burdens on state finances. Moreover, it has also to some degree affected the growth of state-owned assets. It has been estimated that the growth rate of state-owned assets in 1993 was 16 percent, far lower than the growth rate of 38 percent for personal financial assets. If the influence of inflation and the interest rate of 4 percent for state-owned assets are taken into consideration, state-owned assets are, in fact, shrinking.

—The unreasonable structure of state-owned assets has not yet been fundamentally solved. The faulty allocation of state-owned assets has caused under development in agriculture, the basic industries of energy and transport, and infrastructure facilities. It has also given rise to a surplus of production capacity in parts of some enterprises where assets cannot be effectively utilized. Furthermore, restricted by the ownership of the departments and enterprises, the circulation of assets has stagnated, resulting in inefficient operations and the waste of state assets.

—The loss of state-owned assets is serious. It is estimated that state-owned assets amounting to tens of billions of yuan or more are lost every year. In joint ventures, for example, the Chinese assets are not evaluated according to regulations and are therefore undervalued. In transforming enterprises into the stock system, the state stock is not entitled to the same rights and the same interest as the other stock. With contracted management, the short-term behavior is a question, with managers living on the current state-owned assets and irregular property rights transactions. The distribution of gains from state-owned assets is tilted toward individuals and infringes on the rights and interests of the owner, the state.

These problems have been caused mainly by the delay in property rights reform. The planned economic system of "integrating government administration with enterprise management" has, on the one hand, resulted in the absence of a responsible owner of the enterprises. On the other, administrative organs at all levels have become the natural owners and managers of the enterprises and taken a direct part in their operation and management with the result that everyone is managing state-owned assets but no one holds himself responsible for them. Superficially, the difficulties of the enterprises lie with the enterprises, but actually their root causes are that property rights relations are not clearly defined, and neither the system nor the mechanisms suit the needs of the market economy.

Another important reason for these problems is the lack of effective supervision and control over state-owned assets. In July 1994, the State Council promulgated the Regulations for the Supervision and Control over the Property of State-owned Enterprises, thus providing a guarantee to strengthen the management of assets and safeguard the rights and interests of the state conforming to the requirements of the socialist market economic system. Therefore, it is essential to accelerate the reform of the supervision and control system for state-owned assets. The direction of reform is to establish an authoritative supervisory and control system which is responsible to the ultimate owner and can effectively appraise and supervise the management of state assets in accordance with the requirements of the social and economic administrations.

II. The Reconstruction of the State-Owned Assets Management System

(I) Proceeding from reform of the macroeconomic system, the management and operating systems must be reconstructed.

1. Delayed reform of the macroeconomic system is a fundamental cause restricting the entire reform enterprise.

The core issue of the enterprise's reform lies on the reform of the enterprise's macro management system.

Only when the macroeconomic system is changed fundamentally, and new management and operating setups are established to suit the requirement of the market economy, will it be possible for the enterprises to reform their property rights system, change their operating mechanism, and exercise their power to make independent decisions. If these changes are not made, and the framework of the traditional system is maintained, it will seriously restrict the reforms in many areas. In the course of reform, governmental restriction on the enterprises in the contracting system, the failure to implement the Regulations for Changing the Operating Mechanism of the Enterprises, and substandard government attempts with the stock system show that the microeconomic system of the enterprises is seriously fettered and restricted by macromanagement.

The many deep-seated problems and contradictions that must be confronted during reform of state-owned enterprises are all related to the macromanagement system of the enterprises and of state-owned assets. The entire transformation of the state-owned enterprise system depends on reform of the macrocontrol mechanism. The current difficulties show that this particular reform is not only necessary, but very urgent.

2. Ideas for reforming the macrocontrol system.

(1) Redesigning the structure and management system of state-owned assets.

—Establishing a unified ownership and management system for state-owned assets. The state-owned assets of existing enterprises are under the authority of the industrial and functional departments in charge of the government, and just who are the representatives of the property rights of state-owned assets is not clear. There should be a unified management body exercising the managerial function for the ownership rights of state-owned assets on behalf of the state. A state property management commission under the State Council should be set up, consisting of department leaders who are specialists in the management of state-owned assets. This commission should manage all operational state-owned assets, formulate and coordinate principles, policies, plans, and statutes related management, and supervise their implementation. An administrative body for state property should also be set up under the commission as the office for handling the day-to-day affairs and exercising the unified administration over state-owned enterprises. After the state property management commission is set up, the economic administrative departments of the government will no longer directly manage state-owned assets. This embodies the principle of separating government administration from enterprise management.

—Introducing a two-tiered structure for administration of state-owned property combining centralization and decentralization. This double-level structure consists of the state property management commission unifying management, coordination, and supervision, and classified management to combine centralization and decentralization. All businesses and industries which are monopolies of and are controlled by the state, such as post and telecommunications, railways, banks, armaments, major mineral resources, and public utilities should be managed by the departments in charge of the State Council and are subject to the policy coordination of the state property management commission. The general competitive trades and industries should not be managed separately, but should be placed under the unified management of the state property administrative bureau directly under the commission. The existing general industrial departments now in charge will not exercise leadership over state-owned enterprises any longer, but shall formulate the industrial and trade policies only, and their functions shall be replaced by the semi-official industrial or trade associations, step by step.

CHAPTER VI RECONFIGURATION OF STATE ASSETS MANAGEMENT

—Establishing multi-level ownership and multi-level management structures for state-owned assets. China has a vast territory, and the development of productive forces varies from region to region. And conditions in the provinces and counties are complicated. If existing conditions in the different regions are not taken into full consideration, and state-owned assets are not owned and managed at different levels, it will be very difficult to ensure the highly efficient management and operation of state-owned assets. It will also be detrimental to arousing initiative, enthusiasm, and creativity within the local governments. In establishing multi-level ownership and management structures, corresponding management commissions should be established in the regions and at the provincial, municipal, and county levels. The local state property management commissions shall then unify the management of the state-owned assets in their own localities.

(2) Reconstructing the operating procedure for state-owned assets.

—In keeping with the reform of the macromanagement system for state property, state-owned assets should be operated by an independent system which should be set up by an independent state property investment department. This department, specially in charge of operating state-owned assets, is not an administrative organ for state property, but rather an economic entity, an independent enterprise functioning within the market economy. Between the state property management organ and the state property investment department there is an equal relationship of authority. The state property management department does not take direct part in the operation of the assets, but appoints its representatives to the board of directors of the department or the management commission making decisions and exercising supervision.

The state property investment departments include the investment companies, holding companies, enterprise group companies, insurance companies, commercial banks, and all kinds of funds and foundations.

—Separating the capital operation from the production management of state-owned assets. The departments for state-owned asset investment are responsible only for the operation of state capital and investment and profit. They do not take a direct part in business management. This ensures specialization and high efficiency in the capital operation. The day-to-day business management of the state assets shall be done by state-owned business enterprises, which are responsible for production activities, reducing costs, improving results, and increasing profits. Most of the existing state-owned enterprises are just such business enterprises.

(3) Reconstructing the macromanagement system of state-owned enterprises.

Under the traditional system the main characteristic of macromanagement is that the state-owned enterprises are directly under the government departments, and the relevant departments of the government exercise direct control over enterprises and even exercise multi-departmental control over them.

Under the market economy, with the reconstruction of the state property management and operating systems, macromanagement will undergo a fundamental change:

—The governmental function of administration over the enterprises is separated, namely, the administrative function of the government as the representative of the ownership rights of state-owned assets is strictly separated from the general function of social and economic management.

—As the social and economic managers, the government's functional departments cannot directly intervene with the enterprises, but can only give policy guidance and direction.

—As the representatives of the state-owned assets, the government has direct investment relations with the departments of state-owned assets and exercises management and supervision over them. It does not have direct relations with the business operating enterprises and has no direct administration over them.

(II) Establishing the state-owned assets administrative system suited to the market mechanism according to the principle of unified state ownership, multi-level governmental supervision, and independent enterprise management.

CHAPTER VI RECONFIGURATION OF STATE ASSETS MANAGEMENT

Assets are the chief production factor of an enterprise. State property management is the first question that must be settled in operating a modern enterprise system after government administration is separated from enterprise management. In accordance with regulations, a system of responsibility for management with unified state ownership, multi-level governmental supervision, and control and independent enterprise management shall be instituted for state-owned assets. The system shall consist of three levels.

On the first level, the state-owned assets management organ should be set up, with the State Council representing the unified state ownership, and multi-level supervision and control by the local governments.

On the second level, we should name the party responsible for state-owned property as the bridge between the governmental state property organ and the enterprises. While abolishing the original administrative departments in charge, and with a view to reducing the cost of reform and utilizing existing organizing resources, China should gradually form the main body of responsibility for state-owned assets with the state-owned assets operation company as its principal form.

As to responsibility for the operation of state-owned assets, the main method will be to entrust the main body of responsibility for state-owned assets through the use of authorization. There is another possibility, namely, the common practice of contracts in the market economy by which the state-owned assets management organ signs a long-term contract with the main body of responsibility for the state-owned assets for liabilities or leasing, thus entrusting the responsibility for the operation of state-owned assets to the latter. Because both parties have established their relations of liabilities or credit, from the legal point of view, the creditor has no right to intervene in the business operation of the debtor, thus helping separate government administration from enterprise management.

On the third level, the main body of responsibility for state-owned assets holds the state-owned stock of an enterprise to exercise the management of stock rights in accordance with the principle of separating the operation of state-owned assets from the direct management of state-owned enterprise.

Whether the state-owned assets management system can be operated in a reasonable and effective way to achieve maximum profit under market conditions depends on whether its management mechanism can conform to the laws of the market. Therefore it is essential to form state-owned assets management mechanisms conducive to the independent business operation of state-owned enterprises with sole responsibility for profit or loss, conducive to the optimum allocation of state property, and to the preservation and increase of the value of state property.

For this purpose, the following can be taken into consideration:

1. Changing the property rights structure of the unitary main body of investment.

In view of the fact that investments for state-owned enterprises are all made by the unitary main body of responsibility for state-owned assets, the unitary main body must hold the exclusive capital or the controlling interest in the enterprises after they are transformed into corporate organizations. Under this condition, the main body of responsibility for the state-owned assets may intervene directly in the enterprises, making it impossible for the corporation to become market main bodies with independent operations. Obviously, the unitary main body of responsibility of the enterprise's investors is liable to aggravate the non-market defect of excess monopoly. Therefore, it is essential to urge enterprises to construct a plural and diversified property rights structure.

First, we should form several main bodies of responsibility for the state property in the same business by organizing and developing parental-son companies, and encourage them to make transregional investments and buy stocks in other trades. This will form the property rights structure of every enterprise in which many main bodies of responsibility for state-owned assets, and main bodies of responsibility for non-state-owned assets, jointly make investment and hold its stocks. Limits shall be specified for the percentage of every corporate stockholder to form the internal administrative organ of mutual checks and balances.

Second, we should attract non-state-owned assets stockholders while selling part of state-owned assets and vigorously developing the multi-owner, mixed property rights structure.

2. Establishing the personified main bodies of responsibility for state-owned assets.

In order to make state-owned enterprises assume the sole responsibility for profit and loss, that is, with all their corporate property rights, state-owned enterprises should require that the enterprise's investors take limited responsibility for the enterprise's liabilities.

3. Promoting the optimum allocation of state-owned assets through market circulation.

First, we should cultivate those responsible for state-owned assets into market participants for the specialized operation of the property so that they function as investors and resource allocators, and the motive force for increasing the value of the assets and the mechanism for self-development.

Second, we should develop and standardize the assets and property rights market, vigorously attracting funds from both at home and abroad, and constructing open and orderly market surroundings to gradually advance state-owned assets into the international market.

4. Appraising the value of state-owned assets thoroughly and correctly.

In the management of state-owned assets by objectives, especially in the reorganization of state property, there are two views about the value after restructuring. One view is that the sale and transfer of the state-owned assets is regarded as a loss, especially when the price of the property established by market evaluation is lower than the book value fixed through financial evaluation. Such sales are all regarded as underestimations and therefore losses. The other view is that there is a real and actual underestimation of the value of state-owned assets which should not be ignored.

The first view should be clarified because it looks at the

problem superficially and only from one perspective.

First, the main objective of the owner of the property should not be limited to the book value or whether an enterprises is reduced, but optimum value should be sought for the property on the premise of preserving and increasing the value of the total assets. In this way, the standard market transfers with compensation and invigorates state-owned assets. This will not lead to the loss of state property, but rather improve the operating efficiency and quality of the property and be more conducive to increasing the value of all state-owned assets.

Second, while affirming that the financial evaluation of the assets has a certain scientific basis, we should fully recognize the positive effect of further market evaluation. This is because the market evaluation of the assets (such as auction and competition prices) may cause fluctuations of the prices of the assets, but such fluctuations always occur around and tend toward the value of the assets. Especially in the opportunity costs, prospects for development, the supply and demand of intangible assets, and differential income, market evaluation can reflect more accurately the real value of the stock assets than other evaluations.

Therefore, the correct channel is to use scientific financial evaluation and standard market evaluation together to determine the value of assets. Obviously, the results of these combined evaluations will inevitably vary from financial evaluation alone. For the above reasons, it is normal that the value of the assets fixed through the combined evaluations are higher (or lower) than the original financial book value. As long as it is transferred under fair and standard market conditions, this should be regarded as the normal circulation and optimum allocation of the assets.

The way to resolve this issue is to establish and strengthen regulations for the management responsibility for state property. Such regulations should be mainly contract, interest, market, organizational, and financial restrictions on the corporate representatives of those responsible for state property and the corporate representatives of state-owned enterprises.

Under the effective operation of these restrictions, it is possible to preserve and increase the value of state-owned assets through scientific, standard, and comprehensive evaluation while pushing forward the circulation and reorganization of the assets to achieve their optimum allocation.

III. Constructing the Operating System for State-Owned Assets with the Establishment of State-Owned Holding Companies as the Key

(I) Accelerating the founding of state-owned holding companies is the effective method for deepening the reform of state-owned enterprises and solving their major practical problems. It is not only necessary, but urgent at present.

The reform of state-owned enterprises in China is not only a micro question, but a macro question as well. With the organization of state-owned holding companies as the focus and point of impact, China should gradually cultivate a group of national "seeded teams," vigorously push forward the reform of the property rights system of enterprises, reconstruct the macro operating system of state-owned assets, and strengthen the coordination and internal management of enterprises, which are the important channels for solving the difficult situation and the practical problems now faced by state-owned enterprises.

1. In the face of fierce market competition, state-owned enterprises must do all they can to come forward from far behind and catch up, seeking new countermoves for new development and releasing their large potential energy by changing the old mechanisms and establishing the new system.

In their transition to the market economy, state-owned enterprises in China are confronted with stern challenges. By 1992, the non-state industrial sector acounted for more than 50 percent of the total industrial output value, the collectively owned industrial sector for 38.2 percent, and the individual, private, and foreign-invested industrial sectors for 13.5 percent. The percentage of the non-state industrial sectors in the coastal provinces has now risen to more than 60-70 percent. In the old industrial base of Liaoning Province, state-owned enterprises accounted for only 11 percent of newly increased industrial output value, while the non-state-owned enterprises, for 89 percent. State-owned enterprises not only are far behind the growth of the non-state economic sectors, but their underdevelopment is now accelerating.

2. In the face of these challenges since the beginning of reform, state-owned enterprises urgently need to readjust their structure, heighten results of the scale economy, and strengthen the specialized division of labor and the level of coordination. It is especially essential that they raise their competitive ability on the world economic stage, rapidly occupy the domestic market, and enter the international market.

The linking of domestic and international markets will have a tremendous impact on many domestic industries and their products. Those which suffer most from this impact will be the heavy, chemical and basic industries as well as new- and high-tech industries. These industries make up about one third of the national total industrial output value, and are mainly state-owned enterprises. China has a great number of industrial enterprises long affected by high consumption, high costs, low output, and low profit. The degree of concentration of most industries in China is lower than in European and American countries, and this is particularly obvious in metallurgy, chemicals, petrochemicals, building materials, power, heavy machine-building, motor vehicles, and household electrical appliances. China has several aviation industrial groups, but their combined assets are less than that of one aircraft manufacturing company in the United States. The combined assets of several large iron and steel companies in China are no match for one such Japanese company. China has several hundred motor vehicle producers, but their annual output is only 1.3 million vehicles, fewer than that produced by one subsidiary of the Ford Company in the United States. China has more than 70 color TV assembly plants producing an average of 170,000 sets annually, but the Republic of Korea, which produces nearly as many TV sets as China, has only six complete set-producing enterprises with an average annual output of over two million sets.

CHAPTER VI RECONFIGURATION OF STATE ASSETS MANAGEMENT

In the face of these challenges in the domestic and international markets, state-owned enterprises in China urgently need to readjust the enterprise's structure. It is essential to reconstruct the intermediate operating system for state-owned assets by organizing state-owned holding companies as the vehicle for breaking off the fetters of the traditional system.

(II) State-owned holding companies are intermediate investment organs specializing in the operation of state-owned assets, and are independent enterprise legal persons.

State-owned holding companies, which are specialized in the operation of state-owned assets, are authorized by the state to exercise ownership of state-owned assets, and are in charge of the investment and management of state-owned assets. They themselves usually do not engage directly in concrete business activities, but the business enterprises in which they hold the controlling interest are engaged in such activities. Therefore, state-owned holding companies are intermediate investment organs for state-owned assets, functioning between the government and a large number of business enterprises. It is conducive to the complete separation of government administration from enterprise management to ensure the business operation independence of enterprises.

State-owned holding companies are not administrative organs, but rather independent economic entities. They are enterprise legal persons. The holding company is one type of company and is itself affected by the Company Law. State-owned holding companies are different in nature from industrial administrative companies in China. They have no administrative functions. Special attention should be paid to this point in organizing state-owned holding companies.

The holding company is also called the parent company, and the companies in which it holds the controlling interest are called subsidiaries. The state-owned holding company, by holding a sufficient number of stock rights in other companies (business companies) or by signing controlling contracts, exercises the actual control over these companies. In other words, the parent controls its subsidiaries in two ways: One by holding the majority of votes at the meeting of the stockholders and deciding the leading members of the board of directors of the subsidiary who exercise actual control over the subsidiary; the other is by signing the contracts by which one company exerts decisive influence on another, or becomes its chief creditor, thus establishing actual control.

State-owned holding companies and the companies they hold are all independent legal persons. Although the held companies are controlled, they have their own names, regulations, and independent assets, assume independent responsibility for their civil affairs, and have independent power in making decisions affecting production and business activities. Therefore, in organizing state-owned holding companies, we must ensure the independent legal person status of state-owned business enterprises, and their independent power of business operations, in accordance with the provisions of the Company Law.

(III) The state-owned holding company is an important form of organization for the intermediate operation of state-owned assets. It has its own peculiar advantages and role.

There are a variety of intermediate organizations for operating state-owned assets. Apart from the holding companies, there are investment companies, enterprise group companies, insurance companies, commercial banks, and various funds and foundations. In modern Chinese practice, investment companies have been organized and enterprise groups have been entrusted to operate state-owned assets. Experiments are also being made on ways to organize holding companies. As compared with other intermediate investment organizations, the holding company has more advantages and a potentially greater role.

1. The holding company gains control of other companies by purchasing their stock or by signing agreements. These methods themselves have great flexibility and expediency. The holding company specializes in the operation of assets, but is not engaged in production activities. Since it is detached from production and business operations, it can adjust its investment policy at any

CHAPTER VI RECONFIGURATION OF STATE ASSETS MANAGEMENT

time. This is conducive to preserving and increasing the value of state-owned assets as well as to raising economic results, thus constantly strengthening the national economy. The other intermediate investment organizations do not have the same flexibility as the holding company and, limited by their own business operations, do not have the same advantages as the holding company.

2. The holding company implements the state's industrial policies, and by readjusting investment policy over time, supports and strengthens business and industry. Moreover, by exercising economic control of businesses (such as setting economic policy and controlling financial affairs), the holding company also helps the state exercise macro control over enterprises.

3. Because of its peculiar controlling methods, the holding company can form a very large-scale group enterprise. By establishing second-level holding companies, it can use its assets to enter many fields and run multiple businesses. This will not only avoid the risk of lone business operations for state-owned holding companies but, more importantly, it will strengthen coordination among enterprises and cooperation among departments to gain superiority in the scale economy and increase enterprises competitiveness in international and domestic markets. These are the sorts of functions that other intermediate organizations find it difficult to fulfill.

4. The pre-condition for establishing state-owned holding companies is the transfer of large numbers of state-owned business enterprises into companies. It is especially necessary to introduce the stock system, give state-owned enterprises independent property rights, and totally separate government administration from enterprise management. It is also necessary to establish and perfect the property rights market and the stock market to ensure that holding companies have ample means to purchase and sell stock and make property rights transactions. This will greatly help promote the deepening of the reform of state-owned enterprises and the establishment and perfection of the market system.

(IV) Proceeding from the practical needs of China, and accelerating the organization of state-owned holding companies according to the internal requirements of the state-owned economic sector.

Experiments have begun on organizing state-owned holding companies in the aviation, petrochemical, and nonferrous metallurgical industries. Proceeding from the practical needs of China, especially the needs to operate state-owned assets more effectively and produce still greater competitiveness through cooperation among different departments, China should organize state-owned holding companies within the following scope and fields in the future:

1. In industries over which the state must establish monopoly and control, such as public utilities, posts and telecommunications, communications, aviation, railways, banks, energy, and raw materials. In exercising direct monopoly and control over these industries, the state can use the organizational form of the holding company to hold all or part of their stock or sign controlling agreements between the holding company and its subsidiaries.

2. In those industries in which China wants to achieve large-scale economic results, strengthen specialized division of labor and cooperation, and be more effective in international competitiveness, such as in iron and steel, motor vehicles, and machine production. The motor vehicle industry is one of China's pillar industries, but at present its enterprises are widely scattered and each operates on a small scale with weak international competitiveness. It is necessary to increase economic results and international competitiveness by organizing several state-owned holding companies to meet the needs of competition, especially the needs of international competition after the Chinese mainland market is opened.

3. In high-tech industries China needs to give major support, such as electronics, precision and fine chemicals, and biological engineering. The high-tech industries often require the combined efforts of different enterprises to tackle scientific

and technical problems, and a large investment of research funds and personnel. Holding companies are conducive to integration and cooperation among enterprises under the same department, and conducive to supporting the development of the high-tech industries.

4. In those industries in which China urgently needs to readjust the enterprise structure and the product mix, strengthen technical transformation, promote industrial upgrading, and raise the specialized technological level, such as textiles and construction. At present, China has a large number of textile and building enterprises, each operating on a small scale with outdated equipment, low technical levels and poor-quality products. They urgently need to strengthen their technical transformation, promote industrial upgrading, and raise productivity and the enterprise management level by readjusting the enterprise structure and organizing group enterprises.

5. Organizing holding companies will by no means establish a business or industrial monopoly. It is necessary to avoid business and industrial monopolies in the course of organizing holding companies, to avoid a slide back into the old system. Therefore, state-owned holding companies should try their best to form enterprise groups embracing different industries or trades, and comprising enterprises which already possess important advantages. Some industries, such as textiles, will find it difficult to organize holding companies and must attain optimum results only by relying on themselves. It remains a realistic choice to organize state-owned holding companies embracing many businesses, industries, and a wide variety of products.

(V) To establish state-owned holding companies, it is essential to reform the current state-owned property management system and separate the functions of the government from those of enterprises.

State-owned holding companies are intermediate investment organizations specialized in the operation of state-owned assets. To change the current situation in which the government departments exercise management and direct operation of state-owned assets, it is necessary, first of all, to separate government administration from the management of state-owned assets, or separate the general social and economic management functions of the government from the function of managing state-owned assets. The operation of state-owned assets should be concentrated in one special government organ for management with unified authorization, and the management of state-owned assets by many different departments should be avoided. Therefore, the government should set up a special state-owned assets management commission to authorize, control, and supervise the operation of state-owned assets on behalf of the government.

The relationship between state-owned holding companies and the state is a relationship between the authorizing and entrusting powers. The state property management commission authorizes the holding companies to exercise ownership of state-owned assets, and state-owned holding companies are in charge of operating these assets in accordance with the plans, goals, and policies formulated by the government. The State-Owned Assets Management Commission and its State-Owned Assets Administrative Bureau control and supervise holding companies by appointing directors and supervisors. The composition of the board of directors of the holding company, and the procedure for making decisions shall follow the provisions of the Company Law and the relevant special laws. The State-Owned Assets Management Commission shall not intervene in the business activities of state-owned holding companies either wilfully or arbitrarily.

In establishing the structure of separating the capital operation of state-owned assets from production activities, state-owned holding companies are in charge of the operation of state-owned assets, investments, and profits, but do not directly participate in business activities to ensure specialization and the efficiency of capital operations. The business activities of state-owned assets shall be conducted by state-owned business enterprises under holding companies. Enterprises shall be responsible for production, cost reduction, and increasing profits. The business enterprises shall have direct investment and supervision relations with intermediate operating organizations for state-owned assets, but are not directly controlled by the state-owned assets management departments, thus severing direct ties with the government and ensuring the separation of government administration from enterprise management.

(VI) To establish state-owned holding companies it is necessary to transform the existing state-owned enterprises into companies by making bold experiments in introducing the stock system for greater development.

1. A basic requirement for establishing state-owned holding companies is basing them on the stock system of state-owned enterprises. This is decided by stock controlling methods of holding companies. State-owned holding companies, by using this method of controlling stock rights, hold sufficient stock ownership in the subsidiaries to control them. The votes actually controlled by the holding company at the meeting of the stockholders should be regarded as the basis for the number of stock rights held. This can be either over 50 percent of the stock rights of the subsidiary, or less than 50 percent when the stocks are divided among the holders. To use this method of controlling the stock rights, it is necessary to transform the large number of existing state-owned business enterprises into limited stock companies. The controlling interest then can be held in different ways: One, by purchasing a large amount of stock in a business enterprise so as to hold the controlling interest; two, by dividing the business of the company, and setting up one or more subsidiaries; three, by reorganizing the existing enterprise group company into a holding company; four, by reinvesting to organize state-owned holding companies and subsidiaries; and five, by adjusting the existing structure of state-owned assets so that some of the business enterprises will turn over or transfer their profits to holding companies.

State-owned holding companies can also sign agreements with other companies to form a relationship of controlling interest between them. This mainly applies to enterprises which have been reorganized into companies with sole proprietorship, or to limited liability companies. Since it is impossible to hold a controlling interest in these companies, the holding company can sign agreements with them in which the latter become its subsidiaries. This practice should be adopted especially in businesses and industries in which the state must establish monopoly and control.

2. The share-holding system should be employed to remove the present artificial limits on the current, scope of enterprises.

By adopting the stock system and raising funds as widely as possible, the difficulties of technical renewal and transformation and the historical debts faced by state-owned enterprises can be ameliorated. At the same time, it is conducive to transferring social consumption funds to investment funds. Experiments must be made in many more fields by introducing the stock system in all areas where this system can be adopted. This is especially true of infrastructure facilities, basic industries, and public utilities, where stock system can be adopted to accelerate construction and solve the problem of "bottleneck restrictions." Enterprises of all sizes, large and small, can advance by introducing the stock system. The state monopoly of stock ownership should be abolished and enterprises not owned by the state should be permitted to buy stock and hold the controlling interest to assure the separation of government administration from enterprise management. It is essential to have a correct understanding of the question of controlling interest held by overseas capital, because these investors are always concerned with results and risks to their investments. If they are not permitted to hold the controlling interest, overseas investors will not invest. People should emancipate their minds even more boldly on the question of foreign capital holding the controlling interest in the securities of state-owned enterprises not vital to the national economy and the people's livelihood, and there should be no limits on this.

IV. Optimum Results for State-Owned Assets: Reallocation of State-Owned Assets

(I) There should be major differences under the new economic system in the position and role of state-owned assets.

Under the past highly centralized planned economic system, great stress was placed on the "larger-sized and higher degree of public ownership." The belief was, the more economic forms of sole state ownership, the better; and the larger the economic form, the better. State ownership occupied the absolute controlling position in all areas of the economy, down to and including public bath houses, barber shops, and small restaurants. All were state-owned assets. This produced two consequences: One, the overall economic results were poor, and two, the power of the state-owned assets was not brought into full play.

Under the socialist market economic system, because of the changes in the economic system and the external environment, the position and role of the assets of state-owned enterprises should differ greatly from the old system.

—Diversing economic sectors coexist, state-owned enterprises and the enterprises not owned by the state compete with each other in the market. It then becomes impossible for state-owned enterprises to take part in all economic endeavors.

—State-owned enterprises should not seek absolute superiority by size, but rather by results achieved through competition. As long as state-owned assets demonstrate maximum and optimum profitability, their role is fully realized. There is no need for state-owned enterprises to control all facets of the economy to have a leading role.

—More importantly, state-owned assets can not only preserve and increase their value in the general sense, but should also consider their role in the overall interest, the local interest and the long-term interest of the national economy. In the market economy itself, there are contradictions between local and overall interests, between immediate and long-term interests, and between private and social interests. When the other participants in the market concentrate their production in general competitive economic areas having a short cycle and quick results with high profits, state-owned enterprises should proceed with the sustained, fast, stable, and coordinated development of the national economy. They should concentrate state-owned assets mainly in the basic industries with a long cycle and slower results and key industries vital to the national economy and the people's livelihood.

(II) **Under the market economy, state-owned assets are judged mainly by basic results, founded on establishing a leading position and quality of service.**

—Basic results in the development of the national economy. These are mainly reflected in the use of state-owned assets for the development of infrastructure facilities and basic industries. The development of the infrastructure and basic industries to a large degree decides the long-term development of the entire national economy. Considering overall and long-term results, large-scale commitment of state-owned assets should be concentrated in infrastructure facilities and basic industries to lay a firm foundation for the development of the national economy as a whole.

—The results of a leading position in key economic areas. We practise a socialist market economy, and under the premise of equal competition, state-owned assets should and must take the leading role in some industries and fields such as banking, insurance, posts and telecommunications, communications, aerospace, and aviation.

—The results of public services. As to public utilities and the cultural undertakings of society, although there remains the question of economic results, greater consideration should be given to the social results. Proceeding from the overall interests of society, state-owned assets should be duty bound to play an important role in these fields. At present, public services and educational and cultural undertakings in Chinese society are still underdeveloped and can hardly meet the needs of economic and social development. More state-owned assets should be invested in these fields.

CHAPTER VI RECONFIGURATION OF STATE ASSETS MANAGEMENT

(III) Make optimum allocations of state-owned assets through the market mechanisms to adjust the structure of these assets and the structure of state-owned enterprises.

To seek optimum results for state-owned assets, we should adjust the structure of the assets and gradually reduce their proportion in general competitive trades. General competitive trades are those economic fields which can attract funds and overseas capital more easily. An over-concentration of capital accumulation in the general competitive trades will lead to a partial and irrational allocation of the economic resources of society, and to the waste and loss of resources. In order to ensure full development of infrastructure facilities, basic industries and public utilities in China, and to make the optimum allocation of resources, give maximum play to the role of state-owned assets, and to create a good investment environments for non-state-owned assets, state-owned assets of China should be shifted from the general competitive trades to the basic industries and non-competitive trades.

The gradual reduction of the proportion of state-owned assets in the general competitive trades does not mean there is no competition in the operation of these assets. Under the market economy, competition must exist. First, state-owned assets are not exempt from competition, but take an active part in competitive trades and fields vital to the national economy and the people's livelihood and where state-owned economic sector must take the leading position. Second, state-owned assets will be operated through competition to improve efficiency and results in the basic industries and public utilities, with special investment from state-owned assets. State-owned assets can compete either with non-state assets or with each other. Third, competition among state-owned assets should be appropriate in the basic industries and public utilities to avoid the regional and departmental division of the assets, multiple ownership, redundant construction, and a new imbalance in the allocation of resources.

Under the planned economic system, the allocation of state-owned assets was made by mandatory planning and administrative mechanisms. Under the market economic system, the reallocation of state-owned assets and the readjustment of the structure of these assets must be made through the market mechanisms and under the guidance of the state's investment and industrial policies, but not by administrative means or administrative mandates. Therefore, we must:

—Marketize state-owned assets. State-owned assets must function in the capital market and the property rights market to achieve the transfer and reorganization of property rights. For this purpose, it is necessary to perfect the stock market and the property rights market to encourage the transfer of property rights.

—Set up the backruptcy mechanisms. In the face of competition, state-owned enterprises should also be eliminated like other enterprises if their results are poor. The state-owned enterprises with fewer assets than liabilities and without any hope of improvement should be resolutely bankrupted to optimize state-owned assets and the structure of state-owned enterprises.

—Reorganize bank liabilities. As to the enterprises which must be kept and have prospects for development, the question of their historical debts should be solved appropriately. By turning bank liabilities into stock rights, the debt of enterprise owed to the banks is changed into bank investments in these enterprises.

—Private operation of state-owned assets. In readjusting the structure of state-owned assets, we may change enterprises in the general competitive trades, especially small and medium-sized ones, into state-owned but privately operated enterprises. This can be done by the transfer and sale of the property rights, or by soliciting bids for the right to operate these enterprises.

Chapter VII
Separation of Government Administration from Enterprise Management: The Key to Changing the State-Owned Enterprise System

I. The Roots of the Deep Contradictions in the Reform of the Chinese Economic System

(I) Great changes have taken place in the relationship between the state and enterprises, but the government's function has not changed fundamentally because of the inertia of the old system.

China clearly announced the establishment of the socialist market economic system in 1992. Since then, great changes have taken place in the government function and relations between the state and enterprises:

1. The relationship between the government and enterprises has surpassed in importance relations between the central government and the local governments on the question of centralism versus decentralization. The enterprise's decision-making power also has become more and more important. Increasing the vigor of enterprises and boosting their economic results have become the starting point for consideration. The enterprises have acquired varying degrees of decision-making power in production and business operations, marketing products, purchasing equipment, organizational setup, production arrangements, appointment and removal of personnel, and labor and wages.

2. The state monopoly on the revenues and expenditures of enterprises has been ended, and the distribution relationship

between the state and enterprises has been fundamentally altered.

3. Enterprises are gradually becoming commodity producers and business units in the true sense.

4. Enterprises have changed their sole dependence on the government to a dual dependence on the government and the market, and are gradually changing to depending mainly on the market.

5. The government function of vertical administrative intervention in enterprises has been greatly weakened. Direct administrative intervention in production and business activities of enterprises is no longer regarded as a matter of course. All relations between the government and enterprises are more and more becoming governed by the legal system.

However, because of the inertia of the old system, there are still remaining problems:

1. The combination of duties and responsibilities between the government and enterprises. Very often, it is either the government in place of enterprises or enterprises in place of the government.

2. The fusion of the function of property rights management with the function of administrative management. The governmental management of enterprises in a trade or industry is exercised mainly through the department in charge, which often directly intervenes in the internal production and business activities of enterprises, making it difficult to separate the functions of the government from those of enterprises.

3. Non-separation of investments and loans. This not only is a question of ownership of the property rights of enterprises assets, but also a question of enterprise debt structure.

So far as the ownership of the property rights of enterprise assets is concerned, there are two scenarios:

(1) Loans received by original state-owned enterprises. In general, the government had investments in all state-owned enterprises, and the original investments were all made by the government. Under these conditions, the assets formed after the loans were repaid, whether before or after taxes were all be owned by the government, and the property rights belonged to the

CHAPTER VII SEPARATING ADMINISTRATION FROM MANAGEMENT

government.

(2) The loans issued to new state-owned enterprises. The government made no primary investments in these enterprises, and all the funds of these enterprises come from loans. If these enterprises are permitted to repay the loans before taxes, the amount of money equal to the tax paid to the government is used as the original investment in the enterprises, and the enterprise should be owned by the state. If the enterprise is asked to pay back the loan after taxes, this enterprise cannot be called a state-owned enterprise, but is owned by all its employees. It is a collectively owned enterprise.

So far as the finance structure of the enterprise is concerned, whether old or new state-owned enterprises, whether they repay the loans before or after taxes, the investments and loans are not separated, worsening the financial structure. The rate of liability of enterprises is generally too high, and the rate of liability for new state-owned enterprises is often 100 percent of their assets.

4. The operations of the government organs have difficulty meeting the requirements of a market economy.

The reform of the Chinese economic system is being made with the increased vigour of these enterprises as the central goal. In more than 10 years of reform, it has always been the focal point to increase the vigour of enterprises and to invigorate the management of large and medium-sized enterprises. Objectively speaking, the strength of state-owned enterprises has increased and the management system has also been changed to a certain degree. However, the problem of increasing the vigour of state-owned enterprises, especially large and medium-sized enterprises, has not been fully solved, and the operating mechanism of enterprises has not been changed. The large and medium-sized enterprises especially have not yet shaken off their status as an appendage of the government under the old system. Compared with township enterprises, foreign-invested and urban collective enterprises, the economic results of large and medium-sized enterprises are obviously not good, their development is slow, and they have no reserve strength. At present, one third of all state-owned enterprises operate at a loss, and another one third have hidden losses, thus fettering the economic development of China. However, state-owned enterprises exist in fact. What is more important, they hold a significant place in the Chinese economy and form its fundamental basis and main pillar. China now has about 420,000 enterprises of all types, including 17,000 large and medium-sized state-owned enterprises, accounting for 4 percent of the total number, but with a total industrial output value making up 50 percent of the nation's total industrial output value. To change this situation, state-owned enterprises must be oriented toward the market, and the government departments should not have too much administrative intervention in the enterprises.

(II) It has been difficult to solve the problem of the integration of government administration with enterprise because these are conditions at a deep level of the system on which the government departments rely to take administrative intervention.

1. As the representative of the asset owner, the government has dual expectations from the reform of state-owned enterprises.

On the one hand, the government expects greater returns on assets by deepening reform of enterprises. On the other, it fears that after state-owned enterprises are no longer administratively subordinate, state assets will be lost and the profit from these assets will be reduced. Therefore, the government expects to extend more help to, take more intervention in, and exercise more control over state-owned enterprises. Such intervention can be made through the unreformed administrative departments in charge, or through the newly established state-owned assets management organs, if these departments do not operate the assets according to market mechanisms.

2. State-owned enterprises still exercise the double function of seeking economic results and running "small communities."

As the administrators of society, the government must be responsible for social stability and security. When the enterprises continue to exercise the function of maintaining communities, the government will logically extend itself into the administration,

CHAPTER VII SEPARATING ADMINISTRATION FROM MANAGEMENT

thus, intentionally or unintentionally, maintaining and strengthening direct intervention in enterprises.

3. It has long been difficult to separate government administration from enterprise management.

One reason for this is that reform in China, began at the enterprise level as the microfoundation, and reform of the administrative system as the superstructure has thus been delayed. It has made governmental behavior contradictory in character. On the one hand, the government, as owner of the asset income, has become the active propeller of reform of state-owned enterprises. On the other hand, out of a motive to safeguard the power and interests of the departments, consciously or unconsciously, government departments continue to improperly intervene in the operations of enterprises. This has objectively delayed the course toward separating government administration from enterprise management.

The other restrictive condition is that construction of laws and regulations as part of the superstructure has obviously lagged behind the reform of enterprises; and the laws and regulations which have been promulgated are incomplete and have not been coordinated, thus hindering the separation of government administration from enterprise management. For example, the Company Law provides a legal procedure for the appointment of enterprise managers by a meeting of the stockholders or the board of directors. But the enterprises wholly owned by the state and the limited stock companies in which the state holds the controlling interest must still follow the provisions for appointments and dismissals of managers. Hence, the managers find it difficult to free themselves from the status of de facto government officials and enterprises are still responsible to the government at a higher level, but not to the law.

The fundamental cause for the continued existence of the chronic malady of non-separation and the difficulties in correcting this is the continued existence of the influence of the old planned economic system and the dependence of enterprises on the old administrative system. To create the market economic system, it is necessary to first establish a new enterprise system and cultivate the market participant's independent character. The separation of government administration from enterprise management is obviously the primary step toward attaining this objective. For this purpose, it is necessary to make an overall readjustment of the economic system.

II. The Government Functions and Responsibilities Under the Market Economy

The main functions of the government should be:

1. To use economic policies and economic levers to plan, guide, coordinate, serve and supervise the macroeconomy.

2. To regulate and control the pitfalls market and keep them to a minimum to achieve the optimum allocation of resources and improve results.

3. To formulate economic plans, specify the general orientation for economic development, decide on the geographical distribution of the productive forces and industrial policies, and coordinate the balance of all these steps.

4. To regulate and control the building of infrastructure facilities, environmental protection, education, social security, and job training to make up for market shortages.

5. To establish the market order, define market regulations, and form the complete market system and environment for rational competition to create conditions for the normal operation of the market economy.

To change the government functions fundamentally, the government departments should change their notion of regarding their relations with enterprises as relations between "mothers-in-law" and "daughters-in-law." It is necessary to make "four changes": To change from control by the microeconomy to control by the macroeconomy, to change from the direct control to indirect control, to change from being the "mother-in-law" to being "a judge," and to change from management in kind to management in value. The government function of being the representative of the owner of state-owned assets should be seperated from its administrative function. The government should

CHAPTER VII SEPARATING ADMINISTRATION FROM MANAGEMENT

exercise management of enterprises gradually through the intermediate organizations of the market, and exercise control of enterprises in different industries through industrial associations. It should use the economic levers of interest rates, tax rates and exchange rates to implement industrial policies and guide the investment policies of state-owned enterprises. Only in this way can enterprises truly become corporate entities and market participants making independent decisions, assuming responsibility for profit and loss, and exercising self-restraint. This is a matter of vital importance to enterprises in the face of international and domestic markets for making full use of all resources, opening still wider to the outside world, changing operational mechanisms, establishing the new socialist enterprise system, and developing the socialist market economy.

Under the socialist market economy, the government has the following eight duties:

In the socialist market economy, the government should not make arbitrary interventions into problems which can be solved through market regulation itself. However, the market is not all-powerful, and there are many problems the market cannot solve and so it must call for government intervention. What must the government then do?

1. Some important projects have desireable social effects but not good economic results. These must be done by the government. Municipal projects rely on the government to make investment or give considerable financial support. Construction of public works like large reservoirs and dams, and social service such as schools, hospitals, and libraries which are necessary for society but are not economically profitable must be financed with government money. Public welfare projects such as environmental protection and pollution control must depend on compulsory and mandatory government formulations, laws, and regulations to succeed. Moreover, the military, public security, procuratorial organs, and people's courts must be financed by the government. These are the major repositories of state expenditures. With increased revenues, expenditures on these public facilities and undertakings will also increase.

2. The government should strengthen the management of precious natural resources and land. These resources do not belong to any individual, but to the state. Land in particular is irreplaceable. When one plot is gone there is one plot less, it is impossible to replace it. Therefore, the land speculation must be well controlled. The government also must strengthen the management of mineral resources and exercise strict control over them. We must not be impatient for quick results and instant benefits, but must take the long-term interests of the state into consideration. There is also common property such as welfare facilities and housing built by the government, and the government should exercise supervision and control over them.

3. Macro control must be a function of the government, beginning with planning. At present, construction programs must be well prepared and approved through legislation. These activities should be implemented step by step, through the efforts of generation after generation. Information, statistics and communications all must be controlled by the government. Services in these fields should be provided to the enterprises and to society as a whole. In formulating industrial policies, the government should use financial subsidies and discounts, and tax reduction or exemptions to support some key industries. Besides this, the government can also make financial investments and issue government bonds to accelerate or slow down economic construction. All this is part of macro control. Another important method of macro control is banking.

4. We should prevent monopoly and protect competition. For example, some enterprises still have some administrative power in their hands. These enterprises are in a special position in the market economy, and this is not reasonable. Therefore, it is essential to separate government administration from enterprise management to prevent monopoly, but it is even more important for protecting competition. Moreover, special attention should be paid to the establishment and perfection of regulations insuring that all enterprises are able to compete fairly under unified rules.

5. Public and economic order must be maintained to create a good social environment conducive to creating trust and secur-

CHAPTER VII SEPARATING ADMINISTRATION FROM MANAGEMENT

ity for both enterprises and workers. It is also necessary to strengthen mediation and arbitration in economic disputes.

6. On the question of distribution, the objective of the socialist market economy is to allow some of the people to get rich first in order to finally achieve common prosperity. This depends mainly on market mechanisms, but final common prosperity depends on the administrative force of the government. In other words, the primary distribution stresses results, but the secondary distribution will stress fairness. Primary distribution is the distribution according to work, and it is decided by the market. Secondary distribution depends on government regulation, including both enterprise and personal income tax.

7. Education must be strengthened and personnel, trained. It is also necessary to continue and improve health care and medical services. These areas will also affect the market economy, and it will be difficult for any individual enterprise to do this, and reliance on the government will be needed. It is also necessary to construct spiritual civilization and give the people a correct understanding of the market economy through the media, create a good social environment, and nurture the new concept of the socialist market economy.

8. We should oppose corruption and encourage honesty. It is not only necessary to try cases according to law and investigate violations of the laws, it is equally important to fill legal loopholes and reduce crimes.

III. A Design for the Separation of Government Administration from Enterprise Management and the Reform of Organizations

1. Changing the government functions and optimizing the administrative system.

The change of governmental functions as the superstructure should conform to the demand of change in the economic base. In this change, the government shall expand and strengthen the social function. From the economic aspect, it should free itself from managing the microeconomy, and strengthen its function of regulating local economies and managing state-owned assets.

Guidance of enterprises by the government should no longer be given directly, but through the indirect method of "the government exercising control over the market, and the market guiding the enterprises," namely, through the adjustment, control, and management by economic regulation and market management departments of the government. It is necessary to formulate corresponding relevant laws detailing the government function and role and the methods and principles for the economic adjustment and control, and totally end the administrative subordination of enterprises by government to change the role of the government from maintenance to development.

The readjustment of government functions inevitably leads to the reorganization of government departments. The answer for this is to simplify government administration, abolish redundant and inefficient departments, and reduce the size of government personnel to change the direct control of the government over the economy to indirect control. In this process, the economic administrative departments will gradually lose the reason for their existence as the original enterprises under them are transformed into corporate organizations. Their employees can then be transferred to the general management departments, and consulting and service organizations and enterprises. State-owned enterprises, just like other types of enterprises, will become "enterprises without administrative departments in charge at a higher level." Under this new system, the small amount of business that enterprises must conduct with government shall be transferred to the general management departments. The greater amount of economic coordination and services shall be undertaken by qualified unofficial consulting and service organizations. The government shall gradually weaken its direct intervention in state-owned enterprises to facilitate the gradual separation of government administration from enterprise management.

2. Constructing a state property management mechanism suitable to the market economy.

As the representative of the owner of assets, the government

CHAPTER VII SEPARATING ADMINISTRATION FROM MANAGEMENT

should not exercise direct control over state assets. It should only use indirect methods and assume responsibility through a state property management system that suits the market mechanism, in accordance with the requirement of a market economy.

Because of the dual system and the influence of the traditional system, the state assets management system can be operated either by the old mechanism of the planned economy or by market economic mechanisms. Therefore, it is a constructive reform task to establish an efficient state-owned assets management mechanism adaptable to the market economy.

3. Stripping the state-owned enterprises of their social functions.

In order to weaken the direct intervention of the government as managers of the "communities" run by enterprises, efforts must be made to create conditions for stripping state-owned enterprises of their social functions. This will increase the internal vigor of the enterprises and create a market environment for equal competition among the enterprises.

4. Strengthening the legal system.

In order to speed legislation and promote the separation of government administration from enterprise management, we should urge the central government to formulate supplementary laws and regulations under the Company Law as soon as possible. We should also promulgate local supplementary policies and provisional laws and regulations. It must be pointed out that during the transitional period, while replacing the old system with the new, we should avoid an absence of policies, laws and regulations, because such a void is likely to lead to disorder and confusion in the economy and provide reasons for retaining the old system.

Chapter VIII
Establishing a Mechanism for the Scientific Management of State-Owned Enterprises

I. The Basic Idea for Reform of the Internal Management of State-Owned Enterprises

(I) **Using the reform to promote management and push forward scientific and technological advances, and establishing a pattern for modern enterprise management by changing the operational mechanism.**

The internal reform of enterprises must be an integral reform, embracing the following eight aspects:

1. Organization and leadership.

Changing the power structure. The stockholders' meeting exercises the supreme power of the company; the board of directors decides important company matters in accordance with company regulations; the board of supervisors exercises supervision; and the general manager appointed by the board of directors plays the key role in the enterprise by organizing and implementing the decisions of the stockholders' meeting and the board of directors, and is totally responsible for the company's day-to-day administrative, managerial, and business activities.

2. Strategic policy-making.

a. An even-numbered board of directors.

The board of directors is the permanent body of power. It makes company decisions after the meeting of the stockholders ends. In order to ensure that the chairman of the board exercises his power within limits, the board of directors should adopt the

CHAPTER VIII SCIENTIFIC MANAGEMENT

system of an even number of members, conforming to international practice. If the pros and cons are locked, the proposal shall be rediscussed and demonstrated or the chairman is final. This system establishes the chairman in the leading position in making decisions when the vote is locked in a stalemate.

b. Enterprise research and development.

Setting up non-permanent organs in accordance with the developmental needs of the company, such as planning, technical, production, and educational committes, and an enterprise research and development institute. Specialists from all fields can take part in discussing strategy, tactics and measures for the development of the enterprise to aid the general manager and the board of directors in making correct policy decisions.

c. Monthly evaluation.

A suggestion group should be set up in every department, encouraging employees to propose solutions to existing problems and measures for improvement. These proposals shall be classified and sent to the relevant departments for reference. A system of "monthly evaluation" of the proposals shall be set up to engender a strong consciousness of participation in the administration among employees and create an atmosphere of democratic management in the enterprise.

d. Crisis management.

When problems arise that cannot be discussed or solved through normal procedures, the board of directors or the general manager shall have the power to use every means necessary to minimize losses. Or a decision can be made by the directors at an emergency meeting to appoint a special delegate to exercise temporary leadership powers.

3. Property operation.

There should be equal stress on international business and domestic business, business outside and inside the industry or trade, soft business and hard business, and the marketing of both intangible and tangible commodities. An all-embracing market sales pattern shall be formed with all employees taking part in the entire process. Also the simultaneous operation of risky business and the synchronized operation of the main business and multi-businesses shall be realized.

4. Scientific and technological development.

China should make use of international and domestic forces to develop science and high-tech products, including the development of high-grade products, sophisticated equipment, and specialized and patent technologies to constantly improve self-protection.

In addition China should upgrade products, promote technical transformation, and raise the competitiveness of products with a flexible manufacturing management system (FMMS) to make production flexible.

5. Ideological work.

China should put ideological work into all kinds of activities with reform and business operations as the focal points, and combine tough management with flexible guidance.

6. Education and training.

China should reform the educational system, the internal management mechanism, the training of teachers and teaching methods, and establish an educational system that suits enterprise development and forms a new educational system integrating education with training in accordance with the needs of the economic development of the enterprise.

7. Employment and distribution.

China should introduce the contracted labor system and a system of varied distribution with a job (technical ability and skill) graded wage scale, and establish a system of linking wages with job performance. Moreover, the wage gap in a reasonable way should be widened to encourage the better performance and promote the flow of personnel. China should persist in the employment of contract workers within a fixed time limit, without fixed time limit, and temporary contract workers, assigning jobs after examinations with the selection of jobs made by employees and management.

8. Employees' social security.

The old state labor insurance system should be changed to a social insurance system with the state, the enterprise and employees sharing the funds, paying close attention to the livelihood, welfare and medical care of the employees, including retired employees and their children, and fully safeguarding and improving the employee welfare benefits.

(II) An enterprises practising the stock system shall follow the pattern of "the market economic management project."

The basic idea of the market economic management project of enterprises is one, to eliminate all traces of the planned commodity economy and fully follow the objective laws of the market economy. Two, to stress the overall application of the law of value to economic management and link the system to international practice. And three, management must be based on profit and efficiency through quantity control, seeking the efficiency of management to obtain substantial economic results for the enterprise. The basic channels to achieve this are:

—Seeking an economy of scale and expanding the production of marketable products.

—Seeking a new pattern of modern management. It is impossible for modern enterprise management to comprehend everything, and management must be exercised at different levels with business conducted to varying degrees of effectiveness. Therefore, we should widen the production and marketing network, make accounting units smaller and allow them to make independent business decisions, assume sole responsibility for profit and loss, and divide the expenses originally borne by the company among subsidiary corporate entities. Moreover, the subsidiaries should turn over part of their profit to the company according to contract agreements.

—Seeking maximum profit for products. The prerequisite for maximum profit is the optimization of the product mix. This calls for the organization and implementation of one technical transformation plan after another, in light of actual enterprise conditions and development trends in the trade or industry. These steps will adjust the product mix and increase the enterprise's reserve strength and development. Also essential is the application of advanced scientific and technological knowledge for the development of new products, the improvement of technical processes, and the reduction of production costs.

II. The Key to Scientific Management: Perfecting the Company's Corporate Administrative Structure

The key to the company's scientific management is to establish a standard corporate administrative structure for the company. It is well known that establishing a corporate enterprise lays the foundation for the development of modern companies. In a corporate enterprise, no individual stockholder can represent the corporation or exercise full powers, and there must be a special operating system to execute and make management decisions. The entire decision-making and executive system is precisely the corporate administrative structure.

The corporate structure is composed of the stockholders' meeting, the board of directors, and the general manager, who make and implement company decisions. Because of the characteristics of this administrative structure, it is possible to assemble specialists as members of the board of directors or at the managerial level. At the same time, the company's ownership is separated from its right to operate the business, thus making the management professional and specialized to ensure that the company's direction suits the development of large-scale social production.

The separation of ownership from the right to operate the business is the principal symbol of the modern company, and the corporate administrative structure is its guarantor. The establishment of the standard corporate administrative structure is of key importance to true improvement in the operating quality and efficiency of Chinese state-owned economic sector.

Traditional state-owned enterprises are, in name, corporate enterprises assuming responsibility for economic accounting. However, because the ultimate responsibility in fact lies with the government, and there is no responsibility limit, the state becomes the sole owner, bearing unlimited responsibility for enterprises. The government administrative departments as the representatives of the state control enterprises mainly by administrative means from the outside, and exercise the corresponding function of the board of directors of the company, while the factory director or manager is the chief executive officer. Because there is no coordination or tacit understanding between the outside directors of enterprises and its managers, the entire policy-making and executive level of the enterprises are unable to keep up with market changes and fluctuations, and at the same time lack the necessary incentive for development and the restraint of assets.

The corporate administrative structure will standardize this disjointed policy-making and executive system with its poorly defined responsibility, and will place responsibility on individuals. This will keep the entire operation and management system within the enterprises and enable it to keep abreast of market changes, thus producing an effective and highly efficient enterprise.

III. The Modern Enterprise System Calls for Modern Entrepreneurs

(I) Establishing a system of professional entrepreneurs and personnel management, and promoting the formation of a contingent of modern entrepreneurs.

Modern enterprise management calls for the establishment of a contingent of entrepreneurs with understanding of the modern market operations. It is necessary to gradually remove restrictions from the process of selecting enterprise managers by the government, and leave it to the market to choose enterprise managers, removing all limits from the systems so that regions and ownership can vigorously exploit the resources of professional entrepreneurs in state-owned enterprises. The market will determine people of ability and begin using them through a competitive process. Leaders of enterprises should not be appointed by administrative order, nor should the system of administrative rank apply to them. The chairman of the board of directors should not be concurrently the general manager. Only the relationship of authorization and entrusting should exist between them. They exercise their respective functions and powers in accordance with the Company Law and company regulations. The system of registration for the managers should be set up. All professional managers shall be registered and given the title of entrepreneur according to qualifications such as education, record of service, managerial grades, and achievements.

Investors in the modern developed market economic countries tend to be short-term, while the careers of managers tend to be long-term, because the managerial personnel in these countries are all professionals. The managers risk their own business career for the enterprises. For Chinese state-owned enterprises, the problem of short-term investors is moot, but finding long-term managers with some market experience merits our attention.

Managers shall be transformed into professionals who are part of a contingent of managers ready to enter the market. The following concrete measures can then be taken:

(1) Set up an educational system for the training of managerial personnel. Set new standards for training managerial personnel with advanced schools offering relevant courses with improved teaching methods.

(2) Set up a management system for the use of managerial personnel. When the enterprises abolish administrative ranks, the managerial personnel of those enterprises are separated from the ranks of government functionaries in keeping with the new employment system.

(3) Set up a managerial personnel evaluation scheme and practice employment based on qualifications. There must be an authoritative organ to objectively appraisal the duties and responsibilities of the managers according to scientific criteria as the basis for determining qualifications. The results should be put into an information database of prospective personnel to be utilized as the need arises. Assessments should be made during the term of office. The personnel and organizational depart-

ments shall assess and appraise the performance of the managers during their terms of office and put this information into the personnel database. This process of assessment and appraisal should encourage the managers to perfect their professionalism.

(4) Define the duties, responsibilities, powers, and interests of the managers through the market mechanism to turn entrepreneurship into a high-salaried and high-risk occupation with adequate challenges and attractiveness.

(II) Perfecting a system for the appointment and assessment of managers.

No matter which form of organization or management pattern an enterprise adopts, the quality performance of managerial personnel is vital to the success of the enterprise. After the enterprise is transformed into a company, the control of the managerial personnel in charge of state-owned assets should be the next item on the agenda. For this purpose, it is necessary to take the following measures to ensure the optimization of managerial personnel:

1. Perfecting a system of appointments and assessments for the representatives of state-owned assets.

The role of a representative when he comes to a company is first of all as representative of the holder of state-owned stock. Because the holder of state-owned stock is often the largest stockholder, the representative is often the leading member of the board of directors, and holds a decisive position. However, his importance should not be decided by the size of the assets he represents, but by the mandate from the state determined by his excellent performance. The behavior of the trustee of this portion of power must be stimulated and restrained by the external managerial system, including the mandate, assessment and awards and penalty systems.

2. Selection of the representatives of state-owned assets, and managerial personnel of state-owned holding companies through the market.

A standard selection of the representatives of state-owned assets is an important requirement to ensure the quality of the meetings of stockholders and board of directors. The qualities of the general manager decide the results of the company to a large degree. The representatives of the stockholders, directors, and general managers are all specialists at the top level. Under the market economy, the competition mechanism must be used to ensure the optimum allocation of the human resources. The market shall be allowed to evaluate and select the excellent managerial and business personnel so that the corporate administrative structure is composed of qualified people at every level.

(III) Setting up an effective stimulation and restraint mechanisms for the managers.

An enterprise corporate itself does not have an independent consciousness. It must rely on a man in concrete form to represent and operate the enterprise. Therefore, the enterprise manager plays the decisive role. The extreme phenomenon of "ownership by managers" in the modern Western companies demonstrates by negative example the key position of managers in modern enterprise. Past lessons learned in the reform of state-owned enterprises have demonstrated that if responsibility is not fixed on a certain person, or for a particular piece of property, it often comes to nothing. The fixing of responsibility is the dialectical unity of responsibility, power, and interest, and the reciprocity of rights and obligations. In order to encourage managers to perform enthusiastically and creatively, encouragement is necessary. In order to prevent managers from abusing power, proper restraint is also essential. Whether by encouragement or restraint, the overall effect is in the interest of the managers, including his reputation, position, and material benefits. Encouragement and restraint mechanisms free from regulation by interest have proved to be ineffective.

Obviously, the rights, obligations, and interests of persons with different responsibilities may vary.

Therefore, it is necessary, first of all, to reasonably divide and define the responsibility of investors and the responsibility for the operation of the assets of the corporate enterprise. This is the prerequisite for establishing corresponding encouragement

CHAPTER VIII SCIENTIFIC MANAGEMENT

and restraint mechanisms.

The role of the assets manager appointed by the investors is that of trustee of the assets. His basic duty is to take direct responsibility for the safety and increment of the invested assets. This responsibility is inescapable. Otherwise, it will weaken the legal basis for the trusteeship of the assets. Moreover, as the enterprise corporate property is independent from the assets of individual investors, the achievements of the property entrusted to him are possible only through the effective operation of the corporate enterprise. The directors elected at the meeting of stockholders also take responsibility for the collective decisions affecting the assets entrusted by other investors. The Company Law provides for an exception: "When it is shown that he disagrees during the vote and this is reflected in the records of the meeting, the director shall be excused from responsibility." This shows that the trustee of the property is first responsible to the entrusting investor, and this is of more fundamental significance.

The manager of the enterprise, employed by the board of directors, is responsible for executing decisions made by the board. They actually operate the entire enterprise established with the joint funds of all the investors. The manager, as the administrative chief of the enterprise, undertakes responsibility for the quality of the enterprise—though not for errors in decisions made by the board of directors. When the enterprise is very large and its stock rights are widely divided, the role of the manager is decisive. Because the manager at this time not only holds the power to operate the enterprise corporate property, but in fact shares the decision-making power.

Of course, these two categories of managers have different responsibilities. However, as they are both members of the corporate administrative structure of enterprises, they must both hold themselves responsible for its interest. In differentiating the responsibilities of the manager of the assets and the operation of the enterprise, the encouragement and restraint mechanisms as applied to the two of them can be taken into consideration.

1. Encouragement and restraint of the assets manager.

Encouragement and restraint for the assets manager directly originates with investors. On the basis of fulfilling the fundamental intentions of investors, and the return from the capital investment vis-a-vis expectations, investors determine an appropriate annual salary. Generally speaking, except for the managing director and non-stockholding directors appointed by the stockholders, no directors should receive salaries or wages directly from the enterprise. The incentives for the property manager can also come in other forms. When he makes an important contribution to the enterprise, the meeting of the stockholders may decide to further encourage him by giving him a special reward.

Restraint on the property manager can also come in two ways. One, restraint from investors, up to and including removal from his position, and two, restraint from the board of supervisors. Supervisors will be inclined to safeguard all the interests of the enterprise.

Incentive and restraint for the assets managers should be standardized. Apart from encouragement and restraint from the investors, they should be clearly defined in the company's rules and regulations.

2. Encouragement and restraint of the enterprise manager.

Encouragement and restraint for the enterprise manager directly originates from the board of directors. On the basis of the implementation of the decisions made by the board of directors, and the results obtained in creatively organizing and managing the enterprise, the board of directors decides on his remuneration and may also adopt an annual salary system. In general, however, the role of the enterprise manager is more direct and intuitive. Apart from an annual salary, the board of directors may also take more flexible measures for encouragement, including granting permission for the manager to hold the enterprise stocks.

Restraints on the enterprise manager originate mainly in three ways. One, the board of directors, who may remove him; two, the board of supervisors; and three, the enterprise trade union, because these managers have direct responsibility for organizing and arousing the enthusiasm of employees to better realize the business objectives of the enterprise.

CHAPTER VIII SCIENTIFIC MANAGEMENT

The encouragement and restraint of the enterprise manager should be as transparent as possible, because transparency itself is also a restraint.

图书在版编目(CIP)数据

中国国有企业改革:英文/高尚全,迟福林主编.
—北京:外文出版社,1997
(中国市场经济研讨丛书)
ISBN 7-119-00300-3

Ⅰ.中… Ⅱ.①高… ②迟… Ⅲ.国有企业－经济体制改革
－中国－英文 Ⅳ.F279.24

中国版本图书馆 CIP 数据核字(96)第 12867 号

责任编辑 胡开敏
封面设计 唐 宇

中国国有企业改革

高尚全 迟福林 主编

*

ⓒ外文出版社
外文出版社出版
(中国北京百万庄大街 24 号)
邮政编码 100037
北京外文印刷厂印刷
中国国际图书贸易总公司发行
(中国北京车公庄西路 35 号)
北京邮政信箱第 399 号 邮政编码 100044
1997 年(大 32 开)第 1 版
(英)
ISBN 7-119-00300-3 /F·22(外)
02550
4-E-3094P